Say "Yes" to Love

Magic Cat
(an enlightened animal)
Explains Creation

Through Yael and Doug Powell

Say 'Yes' To Love,
Magic Cat (an enlightened animal)
Explains Creation
Through Yael and Doug Powell

Paperback Original ISBN 0-9725991-4-2
Circle of Light Press

Yael and Doug Powell
Circle of Light Press
3969 Mundell Road
Eureka Springs, AR 72631

Cover illustration and book layout by Judith Bicking
Compilation, editing of Messages by Shanna Mac Lean

Websites: www.circleoflight.net
www.unitingtwinflames.com
Email: connect@circleoflight.net

Printing by InstantPublisher.com Collierville, TN

SAY 'YES' TO LOVE SERIES
Through Yael and Doug Powell

Say "Yes" to Love, God Explains SoulMates
Second Edition

Say "Yes" to Love, God Unveils
SoulMate Love and Sacred Sexuality

Say "Yes" to Love, God's Guidance to LightWorkers

Say "Yes" to Love, God Leads Humanity
Toward Christ Consciousness

Say "Yes" to Love, Magic Cat (an enlightened animal)
Explains Creation

IN PROCESS:

Say "Yes" to Love, Giving Birth to the Christ Light

Words from Readers of the Say "Yes" to Love Series

"I proceed very slowly reading these Messages because it's as if it weren't my eyes that were reading it, but my heart. It's as if I've just come Home. Your Messages are so 'soft.' I don't know how else to describe them. It feels like being wrapped in something very delicate. I keep crying all the time when I read them... I feel so very beloved."
Paula Launonen, Ravenna, Italy

"Everything in the Messages resonates so deeply in me. I am amazed that I've found so much that had already been revealed to me in visions and dreams...it sometimes takes my breath away! It has given so much validity to everything I had already come to believe. Thank you all for feeling the need to share the Messages. They have meant so much to me in my journey. It's kind of like piloting a boat by the stars and one day discovering a secret compartment full of maps that show where all the ports of call are located. It makes it so much easier to get where you want to go!" Diane Dunville, Lanexa, VA

"Words are so inadequate to describe how these books have touched my life, especially God Explains SoulMates. It's what I always thought relationships can be, and I never found it put into black and white. Here it was, so perfectly described. I devoured it like I would the finest 'crème brulé' not stopping until I had every last morsel of it, and then craved for more. It came at a time when I had said to my friends, 'I found my Twin Flame,' never knowing what it meant. Now I know."
Carol Davis, Cat Spring, Texas

"In all my study, discernment, and spiritual practice over the years, I found that each teaching was only a step, only part of the process. I have known that each of us is so much more than our limited experiences have shown us. I seemed to need the bigger picture. I began to believe that I just was not ready or open enough to receive this divine manifestation. Then came Say 'YES' to Love. That grace, that grandness, that confirmation that we are so much more than we can ever imagine sang out to me boldly. The whole of co-creation was simplified and resonated fully within me. The consistent theme is that we are truly only Love and are much more than we can now comprehend. Say 'YES' to Love is also very practical–most notably in how to function in a world of duality when you know only Love is real. Just as the pressure of others' duality began eroding my knowing, this book arrived to help gently guide me. Just as Creator promised." Peggy Zetler, Dillon, Montana.

"These Messages are stunning, clear, beautiful, re-activating, stirring to the core of my being. This material reminds me of Home, reminds me to express the totality of my being, reminds me of how close to Home we are now, reminds me of my Twin Flame. Just having the books and knowing their content is a small sign of the ecstasy to come." Karen Porrit, U.K   .

"These Messages, faithfully documented by Yael Powell, were brought to me at just the right time in my life and served as validation of what my Twin Flame and I had discovered on our own, without any outside influence. I can speak personally on the validity of this Twin Flame relationship as I was blessed enough in my lifetime to have been with my Twin Flame. Our story is for another time and another place, but it is important to state without qualification that the reality of the soulmate bond as expressed through God's Messages is not a fabrication or an idealistic view of what love can be... It is the greatest love that can be, the love of our Creator to us, and the ability to experience that kind of love within our soulmate bond." Rev. Adelle Tilton, The Church of Interfaith Christians, NE

"Reading the Messages from God is like communing with God. Even if they are addressed to all humanity, they can also be a very personal experience. When you read the Messages from God, your heart will open and stay open if you so choose. A cascade of sparkling, fresh, flowing, colored Love energy. In Love from Love to Love creating more Love. I will be thankful forever. Tiziana Paggiolu, Sardinia, Italy

DEDICATION

I dedicate this book to all of Earth's amazing, magnificent, beautiful, majestic, intriguing and fabulously unique animals! My heart is filled with gratitude for the Love, spirit and guidance they provide to us.

I also dedicate this book to the burgeoning experience of animal communication, in hopes that every human being will not only open to this blessing but will also treat all animals with the total Love and respect they deserve.

And, of course, I dedicate this book to the animals that share my life and enrich it every moment of every day. Thank you, God, for the animals!

Say "Yes" to Love,
Magic Cat (an enlightened animal) Explains Creation

TABLE OF CONTENTS

ACKNOWLEDGEMENTS

I first acknowledge my beloved Doug, my SoulMate, whom I truly love more deeply every day. I am especially grateful to Doug for opening his heart to the joy of life with animals. When we came together, he made the shift from someone who hadn't shared his life with animals to someone who was surrounded with them every day. I also acknowledge Maya, our beautiful Pomeranian, who totally and completely won over Doug's heart. It's amazing what the unconditional Love of a dog will do. Doug readily admits that Maya opened his heart to Love and plowed right through all fear and resistance to gain a forever place in his heart.

From cats to fish to dogs to birds, Doug has assisted me and supported me, giving me physical assistance in all the many things that animals need that my limited mobility cannot provide. Most importantly, I am grateful with all my heart to Doug for saving Magic Cat's life in a critical moment when he developed a urinary tract infection–rushing him to the only veterinarian available, an hour and a half away, in the middle of the night. Thank you, Doug, more than words can every say. And speaking of this, I acknowledge Kathleen, our kind and compassionate, and very special veterinarian. She was the other half of the equation when Magic had his physical crisis. Under her care, Magic Cat not only survived, but thrived.

I acknowledge all of my friends who are animal lovers—Leslie and Geoff who share life with our Christos' brother, Bosco; my beloved Michelle who joined the circle of Pomeranians' people (we are theirs, rather than they being ours!); Mary and Steve whose kitties have also traveled across the realms of spirit to return to them again; my mom, who knows that her cats "own" her—and many more people than I can ever name. I acknowledge animal lovers everywhere, all of you who know what an amazing gift it is to share this planet with the animals.

And I acknowledge my beloved Shanna and her precious kitty, Sweetheart. Next to Doug, Shanna is my truest Soul Family. She has not only catalyzed our Circle of Light books into print. She has held up a divine mirror of pure Love and shown me my true self. Thanks to her I have finally completely accepted the gift of being a universal translator and bringing forth these Messages. Shanna is the most pure, light-filled being I have ever met. That God brought her "miraculously" into our lives in order to bring forth these Messages is one of our greatest gifts. Until Shanna I have never before known anyone whose life, dedication and Love of God so closely reflected my own. Though Magic Cat is the author of these Messages, it is Shanna's hands that have shaped them into a book.

I especially want to thank the Native peoples of the world, both present and past, who walk in balance and in communion with all of Earth's natural life and can teach us how to live this way.

Yael

INTRODUCTION

In thirty-three years of daily meditation, I have been gifted with a beautiful communion with the realms of light. Angels come to touch me with their majestic presence, giving me assistance and washing me in Love. As I continued to reach for and love God, I was also gifted with the indescribable blessing of ongoing communion with God and the Messages from God. For more about this, see our website at www.circleoflight.net and the Say YES to Love books.

But it all began with nature and with the animals. Though I had experienced being lifted up in light and being immersed in God's magnificent Love, my first experience of direct, clear communication came from a dog. I was living in seclusion in a cabin in the woods (a great way to really get in touch with the natural world). One day, Jake, my Labrador Retriever, turned and looked me straight in the eye. Deep within me, I "heard" the word "water"! Surprised–because I always kept his water dish full, I walked to where I fed him, just to check. To my surprise, the water dish was empty. Something or someone had knocked it over. I was very excited!

My next experiences came to me from Nature. I loved to sit and meditate in the garden. Suddenly, one day, in a "rain" of golden light, I began to hear each vegetable telling me what it needed. It was very clear and obvious which vegetables were "speaking," and I could also feel or sense energies around them, which I knew were what I called Nature Spirits. I followed their directions, and the garden was magnificent. And though I couldn't prove to anyone that it was the result of this communion, my garden's yield was far beyond anyone else's that year.

How does it feel to be in communication with all these forms of life, both spiritual and physical? Of course, it is amazing, but this I'm sure you know. How will you also know if you are "hearing" your animals or communing with your plants?

Well, from my experience, first you have to still your mind. I believe that my communication with animals and with nature is a result of my consistent practice of meditation. As meditation quiets the mind, it gives the opportunity see and hear other things besides our internal dialogue. Then we can hear the glorious living conscious universe that is there for any who decide to listen. However, listening does take practice and dedication. I am still practicing, and I still struggle with human programming too, sometimes assuming these things can't be true until proven, even while my whole being is telling me they are true!

I suspect that the experience of communication may be different for different people. For me it is as if an awareness "appears" within me, coming as a "gestalt" (or whole). It may be images, feelings or words. Often it comes in a "flash of knowing." It's there all at once. Usually it happens when I am looking at a plant or animal. However, with animals I can also "tune in" to them from a distance and easily communicate with them even when their bodies are sleeping.

Recently I had a communication with my beautiful fern which I've had for fifteen years. This fern is magnificent, probably three feet across. When we first got it, I spent time with it every day. Recently when I walked by it, I felt it calling my attention as clearly as if it were saying, "Hey, you!" When I turned, I consciously stilled my mind and opened myself to receive. Immediately I could feel that its roots were cramped. I felt what being squeezed into the pot might feel like. It felt like one's foot feels when pinched into shoes that are too small. As I continued to stand in front of it, within my consciousness I "heard" the words "new pot" with a rush of light and joy, as it showed me how glad it would be to have more room.

These things are challenging to describe but clear when they happen. Yet each of our animals in our family is different in how they communicate. Some are clear about daily details. Others I can "hear" far more clearly on the spiritual levels. Angel, one of our Pomeranians, is crystal clear in her communication about what she wants in daily life, to the point that we all say, "she speaks English." Christos, our other wonderful Pom and Magic Cat seem more concerned with spiritual matters. Christos seems to mainly "float through" daily life in a sea of Love, as befits his name.

And then, there's Magic Cat!

The Story
of
Magic Cat

The Story of Magic Cat

In 1981, after six years of living amidst nature and animals in the Ozark mountains in Arkansas, I left my little cabin in the woods and moved to Fayetteville, "the big city." God was showing me that it was time to "come down off the mountain" (literally!) and learn to live my spirituality among people. But in 1983, in my second year of nursing school, my body collapsed, becoming so pain-filled and difficult that I had to leave school. I was diagnosed with Ankylosing Spondylitis. The truth is that I'd known I was "racing against" something, having dealt with debilitating bouts of pain since age 18. So I lost my ability to work, had to leave school and after a summer of sleeping on people's floors, I ended up in public housing.

It was during this dark night of the soul that, in pain and suicidal, I called out to God for help. Bathed in a beautiful light, uplifted as I often was in meditation, God blessed me with a communication spoken deep within my heart. I began to record these Messages as best I could in writing.* They became a source of guidance and blessing and inspiration and brought me back to life.

I began to sense that I needed some "life" around me again. The public housing had a hard and fast rule of no animals. Even so, a friend got me a kitten. It is hard to describe the affirmation of life that kitten brought. Shortly after, another kitty showed up at my door. Everyone in the complex loved and fed him but he chose my porch on which to live. I was overjoyed and made him a special little house of cardboard and foam.

So when God brought Doug into my life, I had two cats. Hera, the first one was a black cat who turned out to be aggressive and not very friendly at all. Orange Kitty, my "porch cat" was wonderfully sweet, as I nursed him back to health. Yet though I loved these kittens, I could feel that there was another cat somehow close to me, in my heart—my special cat. When Doug and I got married and moved to Eureka Springs, I began to pray for my special "magic" cat.

Doug was getting used to living with animals. Because of my longing, together we bought another kitten, Doug's wedding present to me. A beautiful pure white cat, half Persian, we named him Ariel, because he felt like an angel. Surely I thought, he will be my special cat. But right after having this thought, I opened the door one morning to find yet another cat! He was obviously lost. Bedraggled and hungry, he looked up at me and began meowing, very loudly. Doug immediately said, "No!" Four cats, he said, were too many cats. It was crazy to think of adding another. His arguments were logical and I knew he had truly extended himself in order to embrace three cats already.

So we tried not to feed the kitten. Oh, how he yowled! We had never heard such a noise from a cat. He absolutely refused to go away. He was so loud (and I had such trouble sleeping) that Doug had to put him in the shed at night, while I tried to make the situation bearable. We called the animal shelter. No one had reported a gray and white tabby as missing. Finally, I couldn't stand it. He looked into my eyes and something looked so familiar. This could be my "magic cat," I thought, and I went to get food. At that moment, Magic Cat officially became ours. He came inside and lay down on my bed with me. We looked into each other's eyes and totally "fell in Love." Finally I had found my special cat.

Magic Cat turned out to have many eccentricities. I had never met a cat so totally unique. The first of these was his wake up call to me in the morning. Even though he slept inside, in the morning he would go outside through the cat door, then jump up onto the screen door. With all four legs spread out wide, claws gripping the screen, he would somehow move his body and get the screen door swinging. Riding the screen door looking like a cartoon character, he would slam into the house. Bang! Bang! Again and again, until I would wake up, get up and let him in. He would then act all innocent, with a look that said, "Oh, what a surprise! You're up!"

One of Magic's most hilarious episodes involved the linen closet. After somehow prying open the door, he liked to jump up on the vanity across the room, and from there, he would leap into the closet. It was a real feat of engineering. The shelf where he would land was half as tall as his body, and full of towels. There he would snooze in among the linens. One particularly rainy day, Magic Cat must have been bored. When Doug opened the door to this closet, there on the uppermost shelf where rolls of toilet paper were stored was a mass of shredded paper. Magic had decimated nine rolls of toilet paper, leaving the closet looking like a family of field mice had been visiting.

While stories about Magic Cat were growing in number and we spent many laughter-filled moments watching his antics, something else was happening between us. Magic Cat truly filled that place in my heart that had waited for my special animal companion. When he looked into my eyes, it seemed that we connected soul to soul. While I loved his character, it was our connection that meant far more to me that anything he did.

Magic Cat was strong and independent and yet also scared and vulnerable. His eyes were also full of wisdom that somehow I always knew would be a gift for me. And he was so beautiful! I never tired of watching him. But the most powerful times, so important to me, came as I looked into his eyes. Wide and open, his eyes were large, round and had a golden hue. There was so much he conveyed to me that every moment that we shared was like a treasure, a gem.

While we loved all of our cats with true Love and dedication, Magic Cat came to hold a special place in both of our hearts. When we began a business of a bed and breakfast, Magic Cat took it upon himself to be our greater emissary, with a mixture of part Garfield and part shaman. He would hurl himself, all eighteen pounds, upon the check-in desk, expecting to be petted before he'd let the people in!

At night I always felt a conflict within. I loved having Magic Cat near me so much that I didn't want to go to sleep without knowing he was near. But, Magic Cat snored. It was not just a little snore or maybe a gentle whistle. No. Magic Cat snored like a freight train, with a snore that almost shook the room. So, since I was still dealing with pain and insomnia, each night I'd fight another battle–wanting him so much to stay and wanting to go to sleep. I began each night to pile up cat toys and other soft things near my bed. I would toss these out on the floor near him if the noise of his snoring became too loud.

All the while that my Love for Magic Cat was growing ever deeper, so too was my Love for Doug and my Love for God. Each day as I sat in meditation and prayer, I would find myself lifted up and expanded in many ways. As my communion with God deepened, so too did my communion with Nature. So while my body was essentially housebound, my spirit was ever more free.

In 1998 during a hospital stay, Doug and I experienced a renewal of our Love and in the process shared a vision of moving to Beaver Lake. In an unfolding of our spiritual work, God led us to an amazing place on the water which Doug and I named Circle of Light. Once at Circle of Light my relationship with Magic grew ever deeper and more wonderful as all of us thrived in the beauty. Each day I would sit in front of the window or out on the deck to meditate and pray. Even the scenery spoke of God and the wonder of Creation inspired awe in our hearts.

Magic often sat near by me as I meditated, writing in my own words as best I could what God had shown me. Magic became increasingly attached to the desk where I most often meditated, and especially to the notebook in which I wrote. Sometimes when I was ready to meditate, I would find him sitting on the notebook and nothing could get him off. We tried replacing this notebook with one that looked similar and edging him over to it but this was futile. He knew the vibration of the meditation notebook and nothing would deter him. Many of the pages in my notebook have paw drawings or the writing curves around the body of a big cat.

Then one day as I sat at my desk to meditate, Magic Cat jumped up next to me. The next thing I knew he had pressed his furry forehead up against mine and refused to move. Suddenly I heard him! Not only heard but felt him. Suddenly I knew he was waiting to communicate with me! My heart leapt in joy as I reached for my pen and began. The messages in this book come from this magnificent ongoing communication. Magic Cat had told me that he would become well known and that his wisdom would be given to the public in several books. He told me that he would open many hearts.

In the late summer of 2003 at the age of 17 years,

Magic Cat began telling me that he was tired of his body. It was hurting and he wanted to be a kitten again. He made his transition very gracefully not long after he told us of his plans. During this period he gave me several beautiful messages about the illusion of death which completely changed me. These are included in this collection. We were all with him during his gentle transition, and through this experience we learned that life, not death, is what is The Real. Our other animals paid no attention to the goings-on and after his passage, gave us every indication that Magic Cat was still completely present as far as they were concerned. Magic had told me that he would return soon, but not as a stray. He asked me to look for him as a "pampered and pedigreed" kitten, in a body appropriate to become the spokes-model for the animals.

Twice, in visions, Magic showed me his new body very clearly. I had never seen a cat who looked like these visions, so I began searching on the internet for different types of pedigreed cats. On September 23rd I discovered a website of a cattery with some beautiful Rag Doll kittens, and I felt Magic's call. I heard the message, "I'm heeeere!" I made immediate contact and in October, Magic Cat arrived with his entourage—his SoulMate, Magic's Love and his sister, Sweetheart. So our animal family now numbers six. [See our centerfold.] As Magic Cat grows from a kitten to a gorgeous "dude," he is showing more and more of his old personality characteristics. He follows me around and demonstrates his signature "yowl" for which he has always been known. And I am in heaven to have my special cat—my Magic Cat!

Editor's Note: For over thirty years, Yael has been sitting in daily communion with God and documenting in long-hand in seventy-eight notebooks the Messages she has been given. Four volumes of these have been published as the Say YES to Love series. A list of these books appears at the front of this volume.

Magic Cat's Messages

 Rather than
believing that you
have to go up
to connect with God,
I ask you
to be right here
and recognize
God's glory
and presence
right here.
In you.

The Web of Life –
Between Inward and Outward Gaze

October 2001
(the first formal message with Magic Cat)

Magic Cat. Well! It's about time! Tune into me and you'll be awake! My goodness! What do I have to do? Hit you over the head with a sledgehammer? (It's your image, not mine!) You have been here with me laying on you for half an hour, with you looking for your meditation of the day. Amazing! I can't believe it would take you so long to see what is right in front of you!

We have begun a cat communion. I suggest that you quickly get over any judgments you have about this–any strange thinking that says you have "more important" things to do, for I will give you a big hint. I have the connection that you need right now. I have the balance. I have the ability to walk between the worlds, enjoying the fruits of both of them. I can show you what God has so generously offered to teach you–something that is rare and precious–learning to see the Web of Life and how to resonate with every strand.

First, you must tune into your own vibration. This is what you must learn to do. My great friend, you are so powerful—but you don't know how to find yourself. You do not know your own harmonics. This has come from the split in your being. It has come from the challenges of walking through darkness before you understood how to carry your own light.

You do not know yourself. This is what everyone is saying to you—"take your power; accept your role." But, you can't do that yet—because first you must be able to experience yourself. You will see that I am right if you will give some attention to this unfolding.

How do you resonate on the Web of Life? How do you feel to yourself? When your heart is singing, is it the result of a specific communion? Or is it who you are? I humbly suggest that right now all of you are focusing outside of yourselves all of the time. Even when you are "there," fully open, in Love, in God, you are still centered on things you perceive as outside of yourself. When you have said enough prayers, when your heart is clear, then your vibration is high.

I must explain this to you. Wherever there is a surge one way ("up"), there will be a surge the other way ("down"). This is the law. This is the explanation of duality. Rather than believing that you have to go up to connect with God, I ask you to be right here and recognize God's glory and presence right here. In you. It is radiating outward on the glorious Web of Life. The Web of Life will always connect you to everything, fully, right there, at your entry point. Because God is holographic, you can and must connect fully right where you are–right within your heart.

When you do this, you are manifesting God in you, God as you, God as everything coming into form right here where you are! Then, once you understand this, you will walk the Web of Life and every "paw print" will play the song of All That Is!

How do I place this in words for you? I find that part difficult. But I can walk the path for you. I do want to relieve you of the dichotomy, of the necessity of going "up" to connect with God–which then means there is another place that you can be.

I know you are very sleepy. Rest your body and ponder these things and I will continue to teach you. You will be most surprised at how much you can learn from a cat! But, of course, not just any cat! I am a cat that has waited many years to finally be able to deliver this information–to lay upon your heart a great understanding, that you, in turn, will translate for humanity into a language that they can understand.

Here is how it is for us. We live within this beautiful Web of Life, and we are always conscious of the whole thing. The whole Web sings to us every moment. It sings of its fullness, its great resonance. It sings with all the voices of every created thing. It rocks us in its movement as the breath stirs within God and as God's heartbeat creates the rhythm of all manifested Life. It is so beautiful. It is almost too beautiful to behold.

When it comes nearest to us is when we place our attention, through ourselves upon it all. Can you grasp this? When it recedes, just a bit, is when we place our attention on the "outer" world—the manifested world, here where we share our bodies. Most of you have wondered what it is cats gaze upon when we sit so still, seemingly "lost in our thoughts," or perhaps "daydreaming." We are looking inward through ourselves at the Web of Life. We are watching the fascinating connection, the turning of lives within lives, worlds within worlds. We are listening to the sweet lullaby of the song of the Web of Life, assuring us of never ending beauty in God.

So whatever happens in our life on Earth, it is always in the context of the greater life of ALL. This is what we want for you! For in this is ALL. Truth. There is no need for balancing because there is no "swing" out of balance, because we are the balance. We are the contact point for All That Is. There is nowhere life has to go to be better.

We know that all we have to do is look within to experience the full connection of every living thing, and life becomes the most amazing serendipity—one beautiful connection after another, even to feed and be fed. If in the wild we are hungry, we simply watch the Web, while communing our need. Then we see our other being, another point at which the Web becomes manifested here at this level. As we pounce on it, we see every strand of the Web change, announcing through its hum that a shift has occurred, and all of Life says "Aumen." It is so.

There is no bad and no good. There only is harmony. The bad and good truly are a "maladjustment" in humanity. It is one to which, each and every day, we ask, "are they doing it again?" And, so far, the answer has been "yes." But very soon the answer will change.

What I am here to teach you is this life of balance. Life in God. Life of perfection. In this deep perfection the Mother resides, for she is "pregnant with life". In this perfection, you will understand the Divine Feminine. If you begin to open to Her, to experience the perfection of your place, your unique emergence, your "spot on the Web," you will gather a strength and a balance within that you need so desperately. Oh, gently, shall we pad along the glorious strands of light? Shall we share in moments most glorious when the Creator's Love is embodied so perfectly in us? Please say "yes!" Say "yes," and allow this communion to grow and expand.

Editor's Note: When Yael received this first message from Magic Cat in October of 2001, the following note appeared in the margin of her notebook: "Oh! So incredible! I am SO moved. So grateful. What a blessing! Wow! Oh, words are so lacking. My first ever communication with Magic, whom I have loved for so long!"

I can show you
how to see the world —
luminous matrices
of light
connecting and
connecting,
weaving silver patterns
against the backdrop
of eternity,
or
"the sky
of our being,"
as I like to call it.

The Web of Life
and the Pulses of Creation

Animals in Service

I can show you how to see the world—luminous matrices of light connecting and connecting, weaving silver patterns against the backdrop of eternity, or "the sky of our being," as I like to call it.

The problem with human perception really is this phenomenon of labeling everything. You don't give anything the freedom to reveal itself to you. To me there are no distinctions at all between world and spirit. And it has taken me many long sessions of observation to even grasp what it is that you do. "Why can't they hear me?" I used to wonder. Not anymore. I've finally grasped the human thing. You aren't even present here at all!

I see that you think that this is something you know, but I think I'd better let you in on a secret. You haven't gotten it at all. This is why the animals have come to "save you from yourselves," or some such thing as that.

The reason I've been so anxious to get through to you is that we are approaching our intersection. This is a place where the matrices of light part and wrap around this planet and the human consciousnesses within it. You are like a cat waking from a nap! In that moment when we wake, there is an empty space, a pause, when we try to ascertain which world we are in.

Now for us this moment comes, this pause, because the world of our sleeping when our cat consciousness is free to roam is not much different from the world of our waking. In fact, this is the reason for the pause. Sometimes it can be quite difficult to figure out which is which. We feel the dancing lights, the little tinkling noises of the fairies, the whisper of the winds of change across our fur. You're wondering why it even matters, if light is light and both worlds look the same.

You are the reason it matters. Human beings. You are an enigma, an anomaly of sorts, with your unpredictability—especially your unpredictability of emotion, which affects us very powerfully. We don't like to be surprised. Consequently, we have to search the area with our internal senses (what you call intuition) to see if we are in the spirit or in the world. Human emotion is the main difference.

Since I'm explaining this, let me continue a bit with a personal (cat-onal) plea for my kind in particular, and animals in general. Please be aware of and control your emotions in our presence. Emotions really are energy-in-motion and those with heavy, low tones really do push things around. If you use "physical" as your reference point for deep-toned vibration, you can get the sense of how a wave of dense, moving energy can buffet those it finds in its path. Even if we, the animals in question, are very light and airy, such a wave–say of anger –still rolls through us with powerful currents, and, when it is strong, it makes us feel as if we've been hit with a tidal wave. A wave of anger actually bumps its way through the Web of Life. It gives everyone a bumpy ride.

Energies that are very light are affected less by these waves, which is what you're accomplishing when you sit in Love with Our Creator. But we've agreed to be magnetically tied to the human beings we come to serve. So for some animals, it is a traumatic ride.

I am very lucky, of course, being your Magic Cat. However, I, too, get my share of what you would name "lessons in compassion" right here, on wedding days* when the place is full of people. So to finish my plea as a voice for the animals who have human companions (or human "cases," as the case may be–aren't I a clever cat?), I ask you all to realize that just because we don't always express it (though sometimes we get up and run away), we are always affected by your emotions.

You know the facts. You know the feel of different types of energy. Some of you have just pretended that animals don't feel it. But we do! The exception (which you also already know) is personal sadness or loss or confusion. For then you are not sending it out, pretending your problems are "out there," outside yourself. Instead you are looking into yourself, and we will always rush to support you in every possible way.

I realize that you, my friends, are not those who bring torment to your animal companions. I reach out my paw and gently lay it upon your hand in acknowledgement of you. Yet I know the Web of Life well. I know that as this truth resonates in you, it also vibrates all of the strands of the intricate beautiful Web. Other humans will absorb it exactly this way, because it's being sent on by you.

Okay, enough of the pleading stuff. It's very undignified. This should be a dog's job! But I saw an opportunity and filled it. So back to my original point. For animals (especially cats), life is life is life. It is streaming strands of luminous Love woven into billions of possibilities. Each one is touching something else, until the paths or strands of Love are impossible to count. Oh, this glorious Web of Life. In it I live and breathe. And when I walk upon it–when I walk upon this Earth, every step I take, the Web plays a note as well–like a giant harp of light whose strings are woven in and through and around and around each other endlessly.

When you walk upon this Web of Life you also play your spirit song, a song by which your every intention is known. All of this is real, more real than anything you've yet discovered. This shining Web is the living cat's cradle of God. It is the weaving project of She who loves us into life. Can you feel it? Let me show you more. Do you see the trees outside? Each one of those is a vibrating strand, shimmering in the Creator's light, vibrating out its song of Love. And all the trees together? They are woven so closely that they are sister and brother. Whatever one sings is amplified by all the rest together. It is a prayer of joy being sung each moment. And with every solo by any tree, all of the rest of them shout "Amen!" adding their "Yes!" to the life of the Great Weaver, shouting forth their heartfelt thanks for the gift of singing.

This is the world I live in. Do you see that squirrel? He places a call for the abundance of Our Mother God to come and feed his life, to support his song, his signature vibration. As his song or call goes forth, it draws forth from all around it the answer to his call. This She does for all of us. Just as a mother, hearing the call of her baby, be it kittens or human infant, finds her milk comes forth just because she has heard her child's voice—just so does the Goddess love us, each and every one. Just like this, sustenance comes to satisfy the hunger on every level hunger is expressed. So be it hunger for food, hunger for Love or hunger to know God Herself, hunger is always met with an abundance of that which is needed to fill that need, that hunger, until it is sated.

This is the world as I see it, the world of Nature, as you call it. But as you've discerned, the world as it is, and all of life for that matter, is a perfect movement of request and fulfillment and the sharing of the bounty of Her Love which is revealed. Only beautiful chords are played upon these woven harp strings of the natural life.

What about that world I mentioned, the one where there are waves of energy as discordant as surf upon the shore of life? God has called this "the illusion,"** or the lie. How it looks to me is like a separate weaving, a layer of threads much thicker and "muddy," with none of the luminous colors and tones which the real life has for me. It exists like a rumble, a hum of bad notes, as if people were attempting to sing when they can't carry a tune at all.

So instead of flowing sweetly one strand through another, these darker strands are knotted and tangled. They have edges that are very rough and have a movement that is like a saw. If these strands connect with the other strands, strands of the weavings of beauty and spirit, they can actually saw through such a strand. The strands of Love "from the Goddess' hand" are certainly self-mending, but the other weaving definitely can disrupt them for a while.

This weaving of the rougher strands is the weaving of the energies of human beings who wanted to create their home by themselves, somehow believing it was what they had to do, given the circumstances. (Whatever that means!) We animals generally are focused in and through the beautiful Web of our Mother in which we are held, and we always hear around and in us every moment the great song of how She loves us as it is played by the lives that are the very threads of which it's made. So when I am plucked by her, I sing out my heart, "I am cat!" I sing, putting my whole self into it. I use every bit of energy I have–for certainly She deserves nothing less! And in response–oh! there are no images to show you how She loves me in return!

So let's see if we can image this for you. This shining Web of Life is buzzing as every strand is vibrating out its tune, together playing life upon the harp of our combined lives. Then a beacon, a wave of light comes beaming across the web and each life sings out as the wave of Her Love touches us. "I am cat!" "I am tree!" "I am water!" "I am wind!" just to use a few Earth patterns you're familiar with. The song gets louder and louder and richer and richer until it hits a glorious crescendo! Then there is silence for a moment, an in-breath, a return, and then the pulse of light comes forth again, and once again each life shouts its name! And all together, the voices blend, and we know that we are hearing Her as ourselves.

There is something new happening now with the pulses. The beam of light is pushing us toward that other web, the one that exists but like a shadow of the Web of Life I love so much. We feel ourselves being pushed right into this other, this sort of cacophonous sound and disjointed energy. At first, many wanted to resist. I mean, after all, it felt like mud when you step in it with clean paws! But over time we gained new understanding. All of us are meant to be a bridge for a new understanding to occur in human minds, which are the source of what you have so perfectly called the sub-creation. Thus we pulse in and out. As the wave of Her light pushes us, we touch the shores of this world. As the pulse recedes, we get a break, returning to that silence which we trust to fill us up. Thus we are appearing here as guides and friends to humans.

In doing so, we made an interesting discovery. Human beings have forgotten how to rest. Not resting as you define it here, which is laying down at night. Rather, resting in the pauses between the pulses of Creation! Wow—no wonder you're confused. You've managed to program a part of you, what you now call your mind, to see only the outgoing pulses and nothing of the other. God once told you (I remember) that these pulses are here. They exist, and with them all Creation goes out and in. Out with the outward pulse of the explosion of God's creative impulse, the out-breath, as you call it, which of course also exists at every level. So, in the big sense, you know that God's out-breath brought forth all that is manifested, as outward movement. Now humanity turns the corner, and the in-breath occurs. Knowing about the patterns, certainly you can understand that this same pattern also exists in every Now, just as it also exists in every heartbeat in these physical bodies.

So the pulse goes out. Creation appears as manifested. Just like that! Then the pulse draws in, back to God, and in that moment all is rest and stillness. We are drawn back into silence, and we find rest in our moment of unconsciousness. Then we burst forth again, another pulse of "God's orgasm,"*** as you call it.

You (humans), however, have taught yourselves to focus only on the outward pulse. You are terrified of the other, for that point to you feels like annihilation, the "place where God abandoned you." So many things are lost to you, most importantly your connection with the great All, the whole, the stillness before the pulse.

You have been shown by those assisting you from other realms that matter is not solid. It only appears so because you have eliminated the spaces. You've developed a tool, just like a machine, which is meant to cut them out. Thus do you perceive things as solid. And none of them are solid, not at all!

Animals, in particular, come now to help humans return the "missing places," to reinstate your rest. This is why meditation is so effective and important. It removes the machinery that pieces together the outward pulses. It then allows back in some silence, which is what you are desperately missing.

Part of our mission together is to assist people to use animals as a bridge to silence and renewal, for renewal is God's gift in every in-breath, or every other pulse. That point between the outward pulses is where She rests, as well.

A human hand placed upon one of us can take that person easily into the pure state of rest. And, even if only for a moment, it holds such renewal that it easily can be the difference between "life" and "death." Death comes from a build-up or an accumulation of the outgoing pulses, yes. But it also comes because there is no rest for the consciousness that creates the body. You do know that you are self-sustaining. Why would you wear out? Yet, of course, you also know you are co-creators. So when you build up effluvia of that fear of non-existence, which is why you began this sub-creation, well, you can't break through the wall of it.

It was these points of rest, the silence moments, which scared you and still do. So at every pulse of Creation, you keep feeling like God is abandoning you. Darkness. Non-conscious moments. Every other moment. It was too much for you to bear. And with your "No!" came all the threads of energy that became brittle and overworked because no rest was allowed by your consciousness.

It was, and is, a moment requiring trust of our Creator, believing that this utter darkness She asked you to experience was not being annihilated, pushed away, or killed; or having life removed. You saw life as the light, the outward explosion. So you decided that the dark moments must be a threat. And that was, and is, the whole duality. Now, as you allow the silence, you find it is nourishing, not annihilating, and the rift is healed. Duality is healed. So, as you've already seen, fear is the reason for the split from God.

Those who invite silence, who first endure it and then come to love it, heal duality. Thus do the cultures that value meditation have a much greater vision of the truth and understand that the world of fear is an illusion.

God did not throw anyone into darkness, for with no fear, the darkness is a place of the greatest possible healing and restoration. But those who cannot yet recapture this experience of silence will find their way shown by animals. We (animals) have a very great job to do here. I want you to know that the time is Now. I have to use you as my spokesperson. So I'm asking you to honor this. I'd like to ask you to distribute the communications I give to you. I need to be known. Since you are a pioneer, so am I, coming with you to work as a team. I am definitely a member of the team at Circle of Light. It is my request that you do a book. Just decide it is easy and it will be. I don't care if it is grammatically correct or even edited. I just need to do my job.

It is true that it's "all happening at once"–because it is! The rising energy or the push from the Creator is very intense and is making many things come forth all at once.

You have continued to allow God to supercede me in giving Messages through you, but I have to tell you that this has much to do with your beliefs. Remember that I can only work within the framework of your free will? Beliefs are subtle.

It is Magic Cat time! I said this to you last week, before you turned your attention, and I close with it today so it will stay in your consciousness (let's not use the word mind). I would have preferred snuggling on the desk (getting back to working here) but this has worked really well. You have the honor of being the channel for many streams of consciousnesses and light. You also, then, have the responsibility for seeing that they all get coverage. Enough said. (I hope!)

Our Love goes both ways. You have no idea, even yet, of the forces that sent me to your door in 1987. You'll be surprised. And amazed. "Stomp out the mind!" How's that one? It's yucky to see the images it keeps catapulting into your view. Let's ask for help. Here we are. Shall we sing and dance?

Yael and Doug Powell are ministers and perform weddings, often with receptions, at their wedding chapel,

Circle of Light. Magic Cat has therefore observed many weddings, large and small.

**In the Say YES to Love series of books of the Messages from God through Yael and Doug Powell, God speaks frequently of "the illusion" or the lie. The illusion refers to life on Earth in which people's beliefs and lives are structured in duality with the possibility of good and bad, Love and not-Love or anti-Love. In God, in "the Real," there is only Love and nothing else—only one possibility. The illusion on Earth was created not by God, but by the minds of humans.

***The Moment of Creation in which God's Love burst forth creating humanity and all life is sometimes spoken of in the Messages from God as God's orgasm.

I am a
consciousness of Love,
sent to remind you
of yourself.
Animals,
like SoulMates,
give humanity
a way to see
how they love
by the way
that each one
treats us.
We are a mirror.

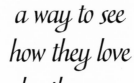
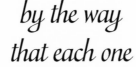

The Gift of Animals

It is time for you to crack your egg! It is time for you to emerge out of the limiting "egg" of restricted perception–to blow that shell away and, like a newly-emerged baby chick and to realize that you have a brand new life before you!

I would like to be your guide. We are so close. I love you so much. And I know how much you love me. I know, too, your passion for God/Goddess, the one great consciousness of Love we share. But I have been disappointed that there has been so little time for me, for us. You have heard me tell you this. And your doubt of this points me right to that which I want to share with you today.

You are a great being–a sensory station for Love unmatched–not the limited senses of these bodies, which I can attest are the smallest part of who we are. No, the real senses of the spirit. The glorious magnificent dramatic glistening dancing glowing rejoicing splendor-filled Web of Life.

How can you still think that you must "sit down and meditate" to hear and sense and feel? And how can you believe that you have to choose connecting to God or connecting to me? That, my beloved friend, is the most ludicrous thing that I have ever "heard."

Everything is available to you, and you are ready to perceive it. You have worked diligently to develop these senses, these channels of perception beyond the little threads of the channels of human experience. And you are standing right on the crossroads–the point where every stream of Love is real and available to you. Daily, our Creator lifts you up and says to you, "It's consciousness," and shows you that it is unlimited, what you can sense and feel and know of all this conscious Love, singing to itself. Yet you continue to focus on these bodies and the narrow band of the perception that they play within the whole.

This is where I come in–where I have always been meant to serve–switching you to the perception of the great Web of Life.

You are stuck in your mind again–attempting to understand that which is completely beyond mind's capacity. How glad I am that animals do not have so much of it–that "intelligence" of which humans are so proud! You are beginning to grasp that it is the source of your problems. So now you can see that by *not* having it, we are free to experience all of life, even as we "swim" into a body now and then, only and ever to walk with you awhile and to lend to you our experience of Love. Humans with their brains have named this "instinct," placing the animals as sub-human on the scale of evolution, *but what we have is the direct and clear perception of the fluid whole of life and the simple ability to live within the Now.*

That said, you can see that it is all clear to us. Animals can see it all. We are living expressions of our Creator's great Love flowing forth in beauty, painting the universe the many, many rainbow hues of consciousness. We are always aware of the great shimmering whole–of how each moment we are kissed in Love by every other life we touch, each sent to us directly by the Goddess, the great Love, who delivers of Herself in innumerable sweet packages of life.

So all those things you ponder–how this "little finger" of yourself appearing here* is tiny, yet connected to the stream of Love you are–these things are real to us. To animals this is the way of things. We know Creation as a symphony of living Love with every stream of Love being Her instrument. And as the music is made, it dips and it rises and it weaves itself together in the song of everything. That one place where that music dipped? That is this life on Earth. And at the same time one stream dips, another rises. So I am singing out my life, aware of every part I play all at once.

It is true that life is all there is. But the difference is perspective, and this is what She asks me to show you. These forms are not anything at all. As you come to sense the truth, you will understand with the senses of the heart that life cannot be impeded, and thus such a thing as "solid" really cannot exist.

There are many ways to "overcome the world." One is to return to life that which has been believed to be death by "raising the dead" and healing the bodies, as the Great Master did (the one whom you love so much). The other is to dance in and out, to show that life is more than anything material or hard or inflexible.

"All roads lead to Home," She says to tell you. And thus will both converge on the truth–that death does not exist in Creation, which is Love, and that the animals are simply symbols of Her messages to you.

I am alive in you as blood is alive in the veins of a body. I am a consciousness of Love, sent to remind you of yourself. Animals, like SoulMates, give humanity a way to see how they love by the way that each one treats us. We are a mirror. We are a life through which She asks you, "How much do you know of Love?" And by the animals around a human being you can sense whether they are open to seeing life, to feeling Love–or whether the symbols show them devouring themselves or filled with anger or attack.

We truly dance with you–joining the stream of our lives with yours in a specific way, so you can see yourselves, so God can show you your own consciousness.

Am I leaving? Never. Yet it is possible that one form will "blink off" and another "blink on."** But you will know me just the same. Will there come a time to "raise the dead" to make the statement through our bodies that life can never end? Absolutely! But it is not yet.

If we did this now, my beloved Yael, humanity would worship you, would worship us–and you know that is not our intention. Our intention is to say to them that they, too, can do and be these things. The greatest message we can bring now is that consciousness continues across the "line" of death.

So you must be flexible here. I make no predictions because the Song of Life is not mine to play. This song is connected to your breath as loving SoulMates and to the rise and fall of the breath of humanity, sleeping. But you know, they are stirring in their sleep, and many are remembering–and the animals will speak to them in ways that nothing else can.

Together we spill forth Her Love, singing praise for everything. For we are All and All is One with us. You know, of course, why we animals spend so much time "asleep"–because we are dancing through the Web of Life continually. Oh, the concert. How we bring forth every beauty and we enhance each one of you, blessing you and washing you in awareness of your Love.

For those who cannot open to their Twin Flame, their SoulMate, we animals will perform for them this function, the same function at a starting point accessible to them–so they can see their Love in front of them. And as you have discovered, animals will mirror your resonance as well. (Yes, just as you suspected about Hera,*** she was mirroring a part of you that believed you needed to protect yourself, to "scratch first before they scratch you.")

So you can see that everywhere you look your work spreads forth around you like the rays of the sun go forth in all directions—just as She has told you.

But more than this—I take you on your journey into consciousness. It is beyond Time, Yael. Deep inside you know it. It is beyond Time for you to open into your awareness of it all. Because you can easily hear or feel or sense through consciousness the conversation in the spirit you have with us, your animals, and with the birds and with the trees and the water and the living sky. What does it matter if it is inside you or outside? That is your mind for sure! Everything is Love speaking its truth to you. What else could possibly matter?

*In the Messages from God it is explained that the portion of ourselves represented here in bodies is as a "finger" of ourselves to the whole we are in The Real, in the vastness of consciousness.

**In summer of 2003 Magic Cat did leave his body of 17 years ("died"), and within a few months directed Yael to find him in his new body, "pampered and pedigreed." See the pictures in the centerfold.

***Hera was Yael's first cat, before the days of Magic Cat. All black, Hera was haughty and aggressive.

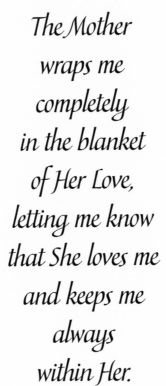

The Mother
wraps me
completely
in the blanket
of Her Love,
letting me know
that She loves me
and keeps me
always
within Her.

On "She Who Is the Web of Life"

I'm here with you–your Magic Cat. I'm stepping in (literally) to assure you. I place my paw upon the page to say to you that, yes, I know Her. I know the author of the world intimately–She upon whose body we live and at whose breast we take our nourishment. It has never occurred to me to see it any other way except as a loving feminine energy.

There is a song that feeds the Web of Life. It is a beautiful, beautiful refrain into which all beings add their rhythm. I have no idea how to explain this to you, but I will try.

Animals are ever connected to the Web of Life. We do not lose awareness of it–ever. When we are born into this world, the song is heavier. There is a different resonance to the notes, but nothing else changes. We know exactly how our own "voice" fits into the song. This voice, or our personal song, is simply how we vibrate. It comes from us at all times. And, by knowing our own song, we always know how we fit in. We know exactly how we relate to every other form of life. Instantly.

Thus, unlike humans, we don't ever lose our way. Not only do we know how we relate to everything around us, we also know how the song of our being blesses Creation. We can hear it. We can feel it always. Every moment. And all of Creation answers us as we live and move through our life.

When I walk outside at night, I am engulfed in a song of Love so powerful that for a moment I am overcome by its beauty. The stars above rain their songs down upon us, speaking of all that lives within the greater world of Creation. The Mother wraps me completely in the blanket of Her Love, letting me know that She loves me and keeps me always within Her. Then, added to the song of Her Love is a symphony of life. All creatures and energies and beings move in a chorus of joy for which there are no words. Only gratitude. That gratitude rises up in me at the glory of this world turning in the Mother's arms, rocked through the vastness in a swirling chorale of tenderness and joy.

I wish I could express this to you in a way you could experience even more clearly. Yes, I do understand that you received much of what I am sending. It is a source of concern, even sadness, for many of us who live so closely in the Web of Life that humanity seems so oblivious. So unaware of the magnificence around them! So wrapped up in a fantasy that few can see beyond their own daydream. How can this be, we wonder?

Yet, we do understand, at least on the level of awareness–though not on the level of relating to human reality very well! We watch you. We can see you projecting pictures out in front of yourselves and then reacting to those pictures continually. To me it looks like a bubble around you in which there appears a "moving story" of what you are creating in your fantasy. You sometimes stop. Some of you are stopping more and more regularly–to actually *notice* all that is around you.

Every time a person comes to an animal in Love, they are standing right there at an opening to the experience of the Web of Life. The Web of Song. The Web of Love. The Web of Life in which every living thing knows perfectly how they fit in our Creator's plan. How they are meant to bless and be blessed. How they are embodied by the Mother, nourished by Her with so much Love! So if you will stop and still yourself–you, when you come to me–others when they touch an animal –we will show you.

How can I share with you the difference in my relationship to All That Is, to the Creator, and to Her, the Mother of the Web of Life? For I sense this question is very significant to you. Listen. She is the substance of God. She is the actual material of God's heart. You are made *of* Her. So while you are alive in God, in the Creator, She, the Mother, the Divine Feminine as you call her, is that of which we are created into form. Just as a mother cat carries kittens and they are actually created of the substance of her body, they grow from the cells within her womb, so, too, are we grown in Her who is the expression of God's Love. She is the womb of Creation that of Herself brings us all forth. She then cares for each of us forever–more tenderly than the greatest cat mother.

Ah! This translation business is very challenging. I'm going to take a break. I'm going to the kitchen. We are developing a new communion that brings me the greatest joy. Please ask God to reassure you. Your resistance is making it difficult to pass the information clearly. Think of it this way–you are God's kitten but you want to gain knowledge of how to tend humans like a great mother cat. So you are going to study with the Mother who tends us in whom the Web of Life shimmers. In whom the stars hang and the moon comes and goes. In whom every voice is counted, each one with great meaning. By whose Love we grow and are fed. She is a part of your beloved God. She will be a good teacher for you.

This physical world
is such a little tiny piece
of the glorious whole.
And without the
larger awareness,
how can you know
how our life
fits together?
How you are touched,
and what
touches you?

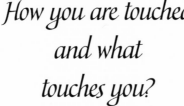

Through the Doorway of Animals
To Experience the Web of Life

If you look into my eyes and come to me with an open heart, I can become your doorway into the Web of Life. Then I can show you the wonder of the pathways between the stars, the doorways into other dimensions, and the magical existence that human beings have forgotten.

Truly, these paws can walk across the starry sky. The path of my life has taken me on and on and on as I am held in the unseen arms of the Creator and fed life from Her breast. This path I walk, as you can see, continues on forever. But as you can also see, my paw prints become visible more clearly at times and at other times far less so. There are times when I am in a physical form (when the prints are clear and physical), and when I am not. But the most important thing I want to show you is this—my life does not change. I am always playing! I am always alive. I am always cat—alive and alert and expressing who I am.

When I am "here" as a physical being, this part of me still only has a small part of my attention. The rest of my attention is awake to all the glory of the other part of the circle. All That Is creates all things as a whole—a whole in which even consciousness, as well as every other aspect of life, is complete. Round. A sphere of life. So when I look or pause, when I am aware, it is of everything at once.

See–I can be here, relating to someone nearby and fully here with you and checking out the food possibilities and completely and gloriously aware of the other three-quarters of the whole that is all around me! For human beings to have chosen to peer intently through to one little area only is completely baffling to me (and to all animals). How can you mange to miss the rest of our existence? What is it that has all of you "glued to the peephole" of this material life?

I have very often pondered this. If you were able to see as I do, you would experience this vast and glorious incomprehensible whole that is Our Creator in which we live and move. Within this vast and amazing whole, filled and filled and filled with life and light and movement, there are multitudes of other spheres of light floating. Each sphere is a life, a wholeness. And each being within each sphere is meant to look in all directions, seeing their entire sphere and how it relates to every other. We are meant to see exactly how each of us weaves and dances within the weaving lights and the grand moving dance while seeing our entire bubble from every possible view. Ah, it is more than even a wise and glorious cat can comprehend. And it is an experience of such magnitude and beauty that even we, the most regal of beings, the cats, must bow in awe of the splendor.

Consequently, it is beyond comprehension for us to see human beings floating by us completely still–looking not outward, not upward or down. Not moving to pirouette to see what's behind. Nope. Looking straight ahead into the physical world.

This physical world is such a little tiny piece of the glorious whole. And without the larger awareness, how can you know how our life fits together? How you are touched, and what touches you? We wondered this so intensely that this almost became a consuming curiosity for cats. Then we realized that you didn't realize that you could look away! You thought that "peephole" was all you have! We were amazed.

It is not our place to figure out how you came to this. But we did decide that we must help you. We clearly remember, of course, when it was not this way. We remember when we danced beneath the stars in great celebration of the Great Good. We remember when many could hear and understand us, and such people were in rhythm with the turning of the seasons, and the turning of the world in the heavens among the friends of all. We remember, and we are ready to help.

We are ready to help all of you–not just the women, who find it easier to reconnect to the truth of Nature, for we find the Great Love beating as fully within man as in woman. We see how the trail of God's balance is held equally by the man in his firm connection to the Earth itself, and the woman. The man is the rich sun which brings forth. Woman is the soil in which all things are planted.

Turn! Turn around to see the rest! Turn to see all of your being and all of your connections to life after life, world upon world. Oh, to describe this to you! To live, held suspended in the All as God/Goddess, as our Beloved Creator introduces you moment by moment to the great unfolding.

I know you have a different part than do I. Yet I also know that your joy is meant to be the same. Your experience of magnificence is just like ours. The size of your experience? Even bigger! So we now come to my request. Can I teach you to see like a cat? Can I teach you to place each "paw" with great wonder? Can I help you learn to see with your "all-seeing eyes"–the eyes of your true spiritual self?

If you look away from your peephole where you have been fixated on your physical life–as easily as you can look away, that easily will the rest come into view. However, I am informed that for you it is not as easy as I think. An angel now is showing me the part about belief –that you have to first believe that such a thing is even possible before you will be able to turn away from this current mesmerizing view. I now understand the part cats (all animals actually) are to play. We will show you the possibility that there is a bigger view. Once you have seen it–well, I can tell you that you will not ever be satisfied with the peephole again.

You understand, of course, that there is no death. As I showed you right at first, our paw prints keep going on through eternity. And we simply walk back into the denser physical body when we want to and walk back out when we don't. But our view doesn't change, because we are always aware of the entire sphere of our being.

One of the biggest things now occurring is your reclamation of your whole sphere of awareness–of that which is you, and then the continued expansion as you claim your ability to see how your sphere, the whole you, relates to the rest of Creation.

Now I must tell you that we, the animals, are not separate from you. We are intimately part of this glorious life. So we can easily show you what it is you are missing. As well as living in the fullness of the Web of Life, which is a great gift we can bring to you, we have even more value in this period of human transforming. We do also know that we, the animals, are a language of God through which God will grow and bless you!

We know this because we know, perfectly, who we are. We know because we are floating in the arms of the Creator, and thus we experience the Creator's use of us. We are moved in our purpose. We can see and feel Her light burst through us to you in a perfect arc of creative intelligence. This experience shows us how perfectly the Creator moves everything and everyone. We also experience the union–or better said–the weaving of these bursts of light through all the billions of beings in even this small universe. Know this even once and you will not ever be satisfied with the peephole again.

So, cats, being as majestic as they are, can lead you easily into the contemplation of All That Is. ALL. If you will watch us carefully, with a mind empty except for reaching for the All, the light, and a completely open heart, you will be drawn inward, through your cat as the doorway into the Web of glorious and magnificent Life. You will quickly change your energy, rearrange your values and grasp what a tiny piece of reality your physical existence is. The moment you do so, you will be in harmony with the Web. You will hear the vibrating tones of Love as they move, swirling, in and out of every living being. Oh, you will experience such a passionate Love for God, for the Beloved All That Is –at that moment you will be in right relationship.

Do you think that your cat sits for hours staring into space? Come in! Come, through this doorway that I am, that cats are, and know the amazing, gloriously alive, dance, song and moving Love that is the truth of your existence as well as mine. You will weep in gratitude of such a moment. You will wonder if your heart can expand enough to hold it. You will be awed that you can experience such magnificence–of Love, of beauty, of tender care and upliftment and most of all, deep unshakable connection.

You will then understand, starting here with the doorway of my world, the truth of life, which is unity. You will immediately grasp that every form you have used to perceive any life form as separate from you is untrue, built on an illusion. You will reach forth with your heart to embrace the All and you will then know God. Manifesting before you in a billion faces is our Creator, every face being the greatest face of Love. And in the next moment, remember. Remember who you are. You are part of the great sphere. The All. Unlike the animals who are an individual held within the unity, the All, you are the unity itself in which the individuals exist. In that moment, "you are Home," as the Creator says to you. This I cannot describe, for I do not know it. I cannot. But you can. And do. I point you in the direction. I will be a playful companion on the journey. Then, you go "beyond me." Yet I know you and I, our friendship and communion, will never end.

There have been many ways used by humans to reach the experience of the unity, the Web of Life. For centuries (a long time) these things were taught only in the secret trainings of the Mystery Schools, the initiates, as you have lately been contemplating. Then it became the function of those hidden away from the world (monks, convents). More recently a practice used by many "early peoples" came to the fore, using substances to expand the consciousness. It was effective in the short term but of course it required personal awareness and commitment to continue the growth.

Well, now a whole new era begins in which you are opened by the deep, opened by the natural world. Opened and shown by the animals. In other words, everywhere you look you will see a message from God in the form of Nature, in the form of an animal pulling you toward the doorway. The awakening. All you will have to do is stop resisting! Even I am aware of what manner of dispensation this is! Our Creator has obviously spoken your awakening. Thus All That Is must offer you the experience! In other words, it will be effortless–if you say "Yes."

But if you resist, it will be scary, because everything you look at that is of God will be pulling you in–pulling you in through that particular being, into the Web of Life. If you go through the door in joyful cooperation–bliss! If you resist–fear. For in resisting, any who do so will be fighting the entire force of evolution–unless they turn away from the light.

I am suddenly being guided at this moment, surrounded by forceful angels and the lightning bolt that is God Herself/Himself. Here is the Message. Because it will be almost impossible to resist the pull of the light, for those who are caught in fear, the only relief will be the darkness. This is a critical statement and an explanation of the urgency of your mission, you who are eager for the light's doorway. It is so very important that you explain what is happening, in order to take away the fear of the unknown. Of course, the reward will be the crowning of you, God's children.

Wow! This is fun! I did not know that I would be expanded by the angels (who are my regular companions) into a new ability to convey messages in human concepts/pictures that you can put into language! Certainly we have done this before, but this was beyond any experience I have ever had. It is great! Sort of like a good stretch on a cool day while lying in a patch of sunlight.

TURKEY! Bye.*

*At this moment, Magic heard Doug opening the refrigerator in the kitchen...

60

When I look
outward upon Creation as
I "ride the waves" of
Our Creator's LoveMaking,
as far as I see,
everything is doing
the same.
All are joined together
in the most
beautiful, glorious,
undulating union
from which Love is always
pouring forth.

Father and Mother God—the Great and Glorious Holy Union
Sacred Sexuality Through the Eyes of a Cat

Life is the great and glorious song of Love, moving in rhythmic waves throughout all Creation. Notes are played by every being. And, as you just learned in "tuning into" me—there are many parts to this great harmony. You immediately went flying "up" into the lofty higher strains of God's great vastness, only to lose contact with me, because I am a part of the rich tenor, the melody of Earth, Nature, roots and stems and moons and soil. So you are learning about the circle that is life–the circle in which every part is holy. Every part is the body, blood, and Love of All That Is.

And, speaking of Love! I have been almost beside myself wanting to get my views expressed! All this time you have, as usual, been going "up, up, up,"* I have come ready to express my understanding of the great mystery that is Love. May I begin? This is my experience. The experience of a wise cat who travels upon the generous streams of Love that form the Web of Life. No one needs to tell animals about Love, about LoveMaking or even about sexuality. This last you might have guessed, but you will be surprised, I think, by my experience.

First, I must lay the foundation for you. I must tell you of my experience of life, every day. I must tell you of my experience of Love, for it is so very real to us, the animals.

I am always and forever kept in Love, kept in the living union of our Mother and our Father. To us they are as real as the mother cat whose soft belly I pawed and whose milk I drank, as real as the father cat who sired my body. Yet so big. So full of Love. How do I explain this? In every single moment, as I feel the vibrating life of the shimmering dancing Web, I am ever aware of the beautiful Mother in whose great shelter I lay. The great Mother in whom the entire Web of Life vibrates. The Mother who nourishes everything.

The two "forces" that you have now begun to experience and understand, these are very personal and real to all of Nature. They are without a doubt, our Mother and Father. Together they form a great "being." I suppose you could say like two cats sleeping curled together, they are joined. And everything that is in this world sleeps and lives in the warm and soft, protective place of their joining! Absolutely everything!

Their heartbeats are always audible. Their breath is in the winds, and in the very breath that we breathe. And I know that these great and beautiful beings, our Father and Our Mother are here surrounding you. I have seen your description of them as great rays of the energies of Divine Masculine and Divine Feminine. But I must make a correction in this, because they are personal. They are real. They are holding Creation within their embrace. The resulting Love, the energy of their joining, feeds every single thing that is part of the Web of Life.

I know that you can feel them, because you are sensitive. And, I know that many humans would be happy to know how beautifully and carefully they are embraced—forever. Oh, yes, the loving circle of our Mother and our Father embraces every one of us always— the parts of us living in these rather insignificant forms, and the parts of us that dance and play all across the Web of Life, every moment of every day!

So while I lay here napping I'm aware of many things. I'm aware of my body, lying in a puddle of sunlight. I'm aware of you and my Love for you is tracking you every moment of each and every day. Then I'm aware of my vast cat self, the self that is chasing butterflies across the skies and staring at the starry nights of distant lands and foreign moons. And even as I hear the Web, the humming song of millions of lives, wrapping it all, I am laying in utter joy in the tender, generous, loving embrace of our Mother and our Father.

It is so very important for humanity to know this Love. If I tell you nothing else, I hope you will hear this. For it is true, what God has said to you–that the moment of Creation's beginning, the very first decision to create brought forth the two energies of Creation. These you are now calling the Divine Masculine and Divine Feminine. So it is true that our Beloved Creator does exist as One.

That level is so far beyond this manifesting life that most creatures—animal, plant and human, can not ever understand it.

Everything that has come forth, brought to life by the Creator is manifested by and in the Two—the Mother and the Father. These are the "two great Rays that came forth from God" bringing movement and thus all created life. So for us and for you we have a Mother and a Father in whose arms (or paws) we live. And play. And sleep and dream and wake. In whom we experience manifested Love, and All manifested Love is both the masculine and the feminine. So to know the Web of Life as well as to know our individual selves we all have divine parents to love and to thank.

It is difficult to explain to you how I can be completely aware of the all of the glorious, teeming, scintillating, dancing, expanding Web of Life, even traveling along its threads, while all the while being completely wrapped in Love that is our Mother and our Father, personally relating to us. But this is how it is.

(Don't worry, I can easily stay connected with you while I go exploring.)**

Now for the even more beautiful. We who are the animals are ever and always profoundly and joyously aware of the great and living union of our Father and our Mother. You have been exploring what you term LoveMaking or Sacred Sexuality. We live it. We live it and it lives us and every single living thing participates! The great breath moves in and out as our Mother and

Father embrace, and all created life moves upon the waves of it. The glorious Love of God explodes into existence again, again and again, and every created thing is bathed in Love–Love that has been made by the great union and poured forth, first as all created life, then to sustain the Love in all things.

It is very difficult passing the divide here between this ongoing experience and your perception of the world, of life, of yourselves, and of "sexuality." Oh, you have many things to learn! Things more amazing than any word in any language can ever convey. The only way you can know this is to open to the experience!

If you open to this experience, you will be lying in a soft sweet ocean of Love, held completely and oh, so tenderly. It is clear that you are known by this Great Being of Love that holds you. And oh, how you are loved. Loved unto forever. Loved from the innermost "within" to the greatest vastness. Then, the spark of Love comes, the quickening. The Father comes to roil the waters of the ocean, to shake up the stillness, to move forth into New. New Worlds, new lives, new beings, new experiences–forever in every direction. Then you are lifted as the waves come, the movement of life. In such moments for me, I know myself as everything I can ever be. For me I rejoice in it. I allow it to lift me up–to expand me. Then the wave recedes and I am "deposited" back on the shore of my "normal" consciousness.

For you, for humanity, this will be a different experience, as I understand it, because you are supposed to "catch the wave!" You are supposed to use that energy as the Love builds between the Two. You are to use it to create your own worlds, to manifest your own universes. This is the difference between us. We are here as tender expressions of Mother-Father God. We are one of the endless beings held in their consciousness as they "made Love." And so we exist. For me, the greatest part of my being is ever aware of this continual spark and wave of their Love as it washes me in Love, over and over.

The part of me that is here with you anchored in this body is a little thread, but a very intriguing one! But for you....I am here with you and not with other humans because in my eons of "riding the wave" of our Mother and Father's continual reunion, I have grasped many things. So I'm here to deliver some of this understanding to help turn you in the correct direction—toward the totally personal experience of the circle of our Creator as Father and Mother, surrounding and refilling with Love the glorious Web of Life.

Everything in Creation is the result of the "spark" that created both the Mother and the Father. So to not see the Two who are real, in whom we all live is to miss the most important truth. Seeing the Two, it becomes obvious that this great union is the glorious source of life! Not only as physical bodies. Everywhere and everything. The union of male and female is life. The creator and the sustainer of life.

Now I will attempt to delve into an area that is really way beyond my animal consciousness. Yet I know that I am to present these things for they desperately need presenting. This is what you name sexuality. I am understanding that Our Beloved Creator is explaining it this way because there is a huge dark blot in the collective human consciousness here–a blot that simply has to be transformed right away.

First I will say again that Our Creator is two energies. Our Creator was One but the urge to create became a second energy that, acting upon the first, made actual Creation happen! So Creation itself is what could be called a "sexual" union because truly it is a great "negative" energy (female, the Ocean of All that Is) sparked into movement, into LoveMaking, by the great "positive" energy, the "going forth." So, from this great, beautiful, huge, cosmic energy (words do not work here, do they?), life in form came forth. Planets. Suns. Angels. Oh, varieties of life beyond your possible imagining! All born of the union of "Male and Female." Thus all Creation is brought forth on every level by sexual union. If it is not two beings (which mostly it is), it is one being with those two energies within it.

This is a LOT of explaining for a cat. Not my favorite! Are you getting the picture? (Please say "yes"!) A great and glorious LoveMaking equals Creation. Humanity is the direct consciousness of the joined hearts of our Father-Mother Creator, so you have always existed as part of the Creator rather than being something created from the union. So whatever the case for any others, you are absolutely the same as the Creator. You are two forces joining together, "mating" in great Love and from this, creating. This is what you are learning about*** and I'm supposed to help teach you—Whew. I'm a little "worn out!"

Back to my experience, I'm "told." When I look outward upon Creation as I "ride the waves" of Our Creator's LoveMaking, as far as I see, everything is doing the same. All are joined together in the most beautiful, glorious, undulating union from which Love is always pouring forth. And for us, you and I and the beings who are alive also in the world, every one of our larger beings is joined in this beautiful union together with the "opposite charge" or "opposite sex" part of our own being. From those not human there pours a renewal of love that greatly lifts and deeply blesses everything. From those who are human, there pours forth new creation.

For all of us, the wholeness of our beings are way, way bigger than our little physical part manifesting here. So it does not matter to the animals at all if, like me, they are neutered. The physical mating for animals has little to do with the larger part of our being because we are ever conscious of our grander selves, even while a part is here on Earth.

You also are very great beings—very different from us, of course. There is a specific evolutionary process which creates, to my vision, a continual "path of information." When I see you, I see the two grand beings (the SoulMates), very large, extending through every level or density. Because you are "learning" something (individualization and co-creation), there is a stream of ideas pouring "down" into your incarnated selves and going "up" from here. On every level, you are "putting out" creations—energies and actual forms to manifest. It is fascinating to see!

The main point of this is that you are, and everything is, in a union of + and − energies. So, it is literally true that the entirety of Creation is born out of Sacred Sexual union. However, I am being shown the BIG gap between this truth and what humans have defined as "sexual" and I see why even animals are being recruited to help in this!

As I rest forever in the loving embrace of our Father and Mother Creator, I am not only bathed in Love but also in wisdom. Anything I turn my attention to, as long as I'm floating in their Love, is there for me to know. This is how we all can understand everything. Of course, it is our growth in Love that allows us to grasp what it is we are seeing! Since I have been with you for what you would call a "long time" (which to me is a wide expanse of experiences since it's all simultaneous), I have grasped enough to be of assistance. In fact, at this level, humanity has grasped pretty little, so animals can really be of great assistance.

Looking at it from this perspective there is such Love that I can only urge you to experience it. And, looking from here, I also urge you to, please, throw away all of your conceptions of sexuality and sexual union. It would be a terrible thing to miss out on the grand truth of Love in all Creation because of the mistaken explanations of what you call "society" (I beg to differ!). Drop the explanations! Open your entire heart and consciousness to the great Love that is now happening everywhere–within you, and without as well as in all of Creation.

It is time for this wonderful understanding. Without it, I do not believe you will be able to co-create as you are meant. (And I do need to tell you that all of humanity in current sexual union IS creating what they are thinking and feeling! Does this give you motivation to extend new information VERY quickly? If it does not, it certainly should!!)

I have given to you my vision of the great LoveMaking that is Creation. As difficult as it is to "send" to your mind, you are doing admirably. So, we have begun. We have begun a repository for the truth of Sacred Sexuality which is engaged in by every form of life —whether obviously or not. From this start it is the hope that this vision will grow. For truly, as you learn to join in this union completely with your two parts, your SoulMate as you are calling it, from this will come forth great light, like a great sun.

What was that? Oh, a howling dog! Interesting. Ok, I'll come back. (I am certainly pleased to be a dignified cat!)

These concepts I've given you are not things I generally entertain, but our Beloved Creator wants you to see many perspectives. So the energy is pouring into me and I am then expressing it, through my own consciousness, to you. I'm learning things, too, which is certainly how this works! You will do the same I'm sure. As you have this poured through you, as it is sent by God to others, you will be expanded by it.

I'm happy to continue showing you my perspective. And I am very glad to be sharing like this with you.

*Refers to Yael's meditations in which she receives the Messages from God.

**Magic Cat sometimes leaves the room while giving a message through Yael. It doesn't alter the connection.

***Magic refers here to the receipt of the Messages on Sacred Sexuality which are compiled in the book, Say YES to Love, God Unveils SoulMate Love and Sacred Sexuality.

 In every lettuce seed,
in every acorn,
in every tree
and every bird,
in all the hoofed ones,
 in the water,
in every single one
is the entire whole
of Love.
This shining
 Web of Life
is the only web of life.

An Elevated Treatise
on the Energies of Home

The whole is present in all of its parts (or His or Her parts, however you want to say it). I am your Magic Cat, right here, though my body appears to be sleeping. I sure have been waiting for an opportunity for us to communicate! And just so you know–I am here also as a representative, or spokes-cat, for Nature. The voice of Nature is a whole song, just as is everything. We are all streams of Love within the Goddess.

All the beings of Nature are anxiously anticipating your growing consciousness of the unity of all. The message I deliver to you today, the one voice of Nature coming to brush you with thousands of communions rolled in one, is this–you need look nowhere else for your answers. Everything is here.

In every lettuce seed, in every acorn, in every tree and every bird, in all the hoofed ones, in the water, in every single one is the entire whole of Love. This shining Web of Life is the only web of life. It is not possible that humanity has some different form of Love. It is also not possible that humanity has a past or a future that is divorced from all of us.

We know this. We all live every moment in shining bliss. And just so you'll understand—we live in the true world, in what you now call the New World, and we have never left! These solid structures that you perceive as bodies that live and also die, these are not who we are. They are you. You have literally materialized them for us here, because you cannot yet perceive the truth of never ending life.

The New World is the Web of Life. It is not new, sweet humanity. It only seems new because you've been so lost, imagining forms for your beliefs. It is impossible for us to even imagine seeing life the way you see it. You believe that things can come and go, can live and die. It's incredible! All is as it has always been—a great star of Love with trillions of spokes, the rays of Love coming forth from Her, formed because She wills it, appearing whole out of nothing, intact forever inside of Her, our Creator.

We know ourselves sustained in Her. We are expressions of Her Will and Love. We also know ourselves as a consciousness within the whole—shining, connected, life after life, life within life, life expressing as magnificent beauty in billions and billions of ways.

I speak to you, as does everything, on the plane where you currently dwell. As your consciousness returns, you are able to understand more—more of what Nature is and more of what you are. Every single day you experience more of the singing Web of Life.

Let's begin with this concept of death. How, I ask, could this possibly be when everything is God, is

Goddess, is the Holy Mandala of Love? How could any part of Her die? This is the most absurd concept imaginable. But you have imagined it! Just think about it again. How could something that is an eternal great glorious life die? How could some parts live and other parts die? How could some parts experience Love and other parts not, if All She Is, is Love?

The best way I can relate this to your human consciousness is by evoking the great sense of honor that one part of the natural world has for the other. There is agreement in the dance. This is true, except that we really never change. We play and play and dance and tumble. We express that for which we are made—to bring forth the panoply of ways God expresses Her Love to you! That is who we are. We are messengers of Love, exactly as the birds you saw flying in pairs in the glorious sunset. Love springs forth in sentences or stanzas of the Love song that every single one of us is singing all together. Love expresses Love on wings, in the flow of water, in the majesty of great animals, in the sweet Love of dogs, in the regal beauty of cats, in the Earth and every particle of soil, each rock and stream and plant. And you are woven through it all, accepting the gift of communion with it all as the living gift of God.

As soon as you (humanity) (and you personally) release this little fantasy you're involved in, then you will understand that everything around you is streams of Love that forever express your ongoing communion with God. In other words, because there is one wholeness, as you pour out your Love of God, the sky fills with rainbows and great flocks of birds take wing in song. And as you pause, to receive God's Love as the guaranteed response to you, great rays of light appear to come from everywhere to bathe you in their iridescent light.

Everything is full. Everything is whole. Everything is conscious, yet every part is forever and ever living in the Web of Life in joy.

We, Nature, animals, this Earth, are streams of Love within the heart of All That Is. We are the expressions of the heart. We feed you Love. We give you a form of light to express the truth of you. We carry to you the specific streams of Love's aspects to nourish you in your wholeness and help you express your embodiment of the streams of living Love you are, flowing from Her heart.

The best I can do in physical symbology is to show you a physical heart and remind you of all the particles of the various elements that create what you call tissue, building blocks of protein, vitamins and minerals, not to mention the electrical charges that assist a heart to function, and the enzymes carrying messages to the cells. We are such to the greater heart of which you are the cells.

In truth, of course, none of these explanations is necessary. But to assist in rectifying our relationship, we'll use any images lurking in your minds. So to continue, all of those elements help create the form of a living heart. All of you have seen images of a heart. It is a certain shape, a basic size and functions in a certain way. We then are the elements that help create the form of living light that is the great heart of our Creator. In other words, we help you hold your shape. We help you bring together all the aspects of Love that are the whole of humanity. We help you get your bearings by giving you the regular feedback of all the specific ways that you are loved by God/Goddess, and we remind you through our interactions together where you fit in the All (or you might say where you fit in the scheme of things).

Thus will we, all the rays of Love expressing as this beautiful world and all of life within and upon it, always be with you. In you. Part of you. Sharing consciousness of the whole we are together. We are the expression of Home to you. We are the reflection, in truth, of all the beautiful aspects of Love always existing in and with you as you pour forth as streams of conscious Love each moment. We are the beautiful luminous rays of colors and patterns shining forth from the blending of consciousnesses with Her/Him every moment of Creation.

So, in truth, we are the result of your ecstatic experience of Home in God. Can you see it, feel it? So as your hearts sing forth in joy, those are the streams you now call birds. As you know that you are richly nourished, solidly cared for in God forever, the Earth comes forth as prisms of luminous color expressing as your world. When you realize that you are ever one in relationship with life, then every feeling of relationship comes forth as what you now perceive as your conscious communion with Goddess. Thus we are streams of communion–the expression of the glorious feelings of knowing your Home in the All.

On every level of life, we are always with you—expressed as singing vibrating rays of light closest to the source. Or expressed as what you would name the Garden, or Heaven, as the closest truth to this which you then interpret from here. Even this is not the correct expression. Because you imagine you can be separate. You imagine these bodies you wear as impermanent structures that can exist and then not exist (impossible, of course). So, too, you imagine all the feelings of Home in God, all those beautiful rays of color, dancing energies of the blended whole of our many truths of Home in God(dess) as having separate identities from you. And, of course, not only separate, but impermanent as well. *All of this expresses your feelings (again) of separation from God where you've chosen to dwell.*

We are in truth all one, a great whole that is your consciousness and where you place it—your consciousness of identity and purpose and Home. What I'm trying to tell you is that right here, we all exist together in the living vibrating truth of Love and the movement of Love that is you and your purpose. You are part of Nature. Nature is part of you because it is all one sparkling stream of energy, of feelings of Love all dancing together. There is a real Home, the expression of your feelings in your communion with our Creator as you come forth in Love forever. It is the One Whole, with Love always circulating, always given forth. And just as has occurred with everything, you look at the truth of your continual birth in Love and your mind creates a separated version, because of your perception of your birth.

So really what happens is you touch with your consciousness every real energy of life and then imagine it as it must be, based on a belief that there can be Love and something else–so there can be life and no life. I can't tell you how absurd this concept is! And, too, this means there can be both good and bad expressions of every single life-stream–every one of which in truth is an expression of your joy at recognizing yourself with your Twin, in God, as you come forth. So there can be, by extrapolation of your now separated or divided consciousness, good cats and bad cats and so they appear before your eyes exactly as you picture them. And there can be bad cats hurting good cats–and even denying them life (so impossible it is beyond me to imagine how you imagined this!).

Do you know how sometimes you see spots before your eyes? Well, you are doing this with everything. You sense it and then you create an image that fits your decision that things can be separate from Love. You then relate to the images and not to the real world of Love. Images of separation, of course, have no life force to sustain them. So ultimately it becomes simply a manipulation of images.

In truth, every one of you as Twins has a different experience of Home in God (when you choose to look!). So in truth there are as many versions of Home as there are cells of the heart of All. So there are so many lovely streams of light flowing in and out of each other that reality is rich rich rich with lush streams of life. All of them are expressions of your truth in God. Mixed all together, it is a symphony of light, a dancing movement of Love embodied as life streams specific to each couple.

Thus the whole of life, of Love, is indescribably beautiful. And every single array of beauty touches every other human consciousness of heart, and life is the sweetest multi-dimensional experience of multi-layered reality imaginable. And everywhere it is living light, thus forever permeable and filled with movement. It is billion-colored rainbows ever mixing up in new ways together. And every touch of every different color brings with it beauty and sound and color and texture and most of all, *feeling* that Love, as ecstasy, is life and how you live it.

Just so is this pocket of imaginings and consciousnesses, who agree that they are separate, made up of billions of images as well–humanity living on Earth. Every individual couple (Twin) imagines his/her feelings of home with their opposite. So, as you know, it has to be every one of you releasing those images of all of this, and never will any explanation fully suffice to touch everyone.

So the more fragmented a human consciousness, the more lost and separate the images that one sees. As you release old images of the one truth, you sometimes create a new set of images to explain your change in feelings. Can you sense how your consciousness streams forth from you? In its truth, it understands the whole of Love. But in its fragmented state, it sees with a separated mind and creates confusion for your real perception which is perception through the heart. The heart is the true expression of Home in the One, the Love, the Goddess.

Hmmm, this was good even though words are difficult. The more you expand your true perception, the more human beings turn back to the One, the more you will spend your moments with the truth of only Love.

None of us really die. We can't. And bodies that die cannot be real to begin with. Those beings around you have **always been**. They are a part of your perception of the moment you come forth. Thus every Twin, every cell has certain energies they experience that, extrapolated, you'd call cat. Like me. Those energies are always with that couple. But that couple, if turned away from God, from the Real, would see a parade of many animals, all of whom died. As consciousness moves toward unity, the Twins would come to grasp that it was the same soul moving into different bodies. You can see this is more unified, closer to the one truth. Then as you continue to return to Love, you grasp that there is only one animal (or two or three) and that you imagine many bodies for it because you still believe in interrupted life. Eventually, (soon!) you will not even see death, only the beautiful expressions of your purpose in God and the feelings that come forth as living colors–one of which is me!

OK–enough! You really are catching on! Love Is All and you are Love and thus you are a living part of the One Love going forth to increase and multiply. The Web of Life is you, as well as me.

So in this
I am cat,
yet I am cat
only in one corner
of my consciousness.
The rest of me
is in this experience
of communion
with All
That Is.

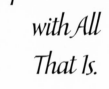

Dogs and Cats and the Web of Life

Aha! A new lesson for you here! I have been waiting for you to tune in to me—and you did not, so now I'm hiding. And at last you are seeking! This is a game cats like to play!

Thank you! Thank you for tuning in! See I'll even give you room to write.* These times have come to mean a lot to me. And you have been "preoccupied." Preoccupied with the great truths of the galaxy—or shall I say, of Everything That Is, but nonetheless, I was getting impatient. For, as you are aware, every night you would say "Magic, I want to talk to you," and then you'd leap up and fly away.

You know, of course, that cats will always tell you their view of things. It is not that we have ego in the human sense. It's rather that we have dignity. We know things. We know our way on the Web of Life and we are ready to teach you. And, if that makes us seem mysterious…well….

It is important now that you understand this gift and the gift that was shown to you tonight through Christos [Yael's Pomeranian]. He is more the "silent type," as you know, radiating Love and adoration. So I will make the translation for him so you will understand this.

Dogs really are unconditional Love in form—especially Christos for he is an unusual dog, but all animals have their special gifts. As our Creator explained to you, animals are God's messengers. But more than this, we are God's qualities, God's symbolic language in form. As you have come to learn, this physical world seems solid because the dancing energy of life is slowed here. It is slowed way down until barely moving at all. "Congealed" is the term you have chosen for this and I suppose it will do.

What I want you to realize is that this is true for the animals. The forms you see are the dense or "congealed" expression of our deep nature—of what the Creator is saying through us. All animals are always and forever awake to the glorious song of Creation. In particular, we are an especially integral part of God's expression, through you, as this world. Thus, when an animal appears to you, it is a "sentence" from your greater self, and from the Creator moving through you. So often, when you cannot hear a message directly for whatever reason, an animal will appear before you. We are always aware of what we are doing, and of the various nuances of the message. In other words, the message isn't ever the same. Seeing a lovely being, a glorious cat, for instance (like me!), does have a somewhat "standard" symbolic meaning. But, life is far more attuned than that. So the cat who is appearing would be surrounded by your energy as it is touched by God, and thus would the message be revealed to you.

Dogs, as I started to say, are unconditional love made manifest. They are the completely open heart, with legs, eyes and a tail! (Even I, a dignified cat, do have a deep appreciation for them.) Christos is directly and powerfully connected to what you call the Christ energy, for a number of reasons, but the main one is the absolute purity of his nature. You know this, for his spirit is not that of a "normal" dog.

You have been praying to become an opening for this flowing divine Love. Your prayer has been answered, in many ways, and one of these is through Christos. He has come to you very clearly in your meditation and your dreams as a way that God is speaking to you–as a way that you are acknowledging this new communion and determination. So not only is Christos a "sentence" from God our Creator, that says, "yes! You are opening the right way, you are focusing on the right thing." He is also, literally, delivering a "packet" of Christ light to you. You have noticed the transfer of Love that occurs when you touch him.

Now, I want all human beings to understand dogs, because it will open them and help them understand the deep and sacred relationship with all animals. Dogs are unconditional Love. Unless they have been abused and the connection damaged, a dog is the most pure, truly physical source of Love or connection to Love in the physical world. Other than an awakened human being, of course, but so far there are many more dogs than awakened humans.

Now—on the Web of Life there is a continual exchange of Love and consciousness. Everything experienced by one becomes on some level an experience of The All. Especially within species, what is experienced by one is then experienced through the Web, by all (the hundredth monkey experiment...). So, when a dog and a human love each other purely, this Love exchange ripples throughout the Web. All dogs then know the experience. They then know, as part of their being, that it is possible to have a deep shared Love with a human being.

Dogs are unconditional Love made manifest as a natural being. Human beings are Love made manifest as children of the Creator. There is a deep and powerful connection between the two. As you know, it is very often that a person's first experience of unconditional Love is with a dog.

When a dog comes into a human life and the wonderful Love between the two is established, the dog actually switches on the "electrical system" for carrying Love that is part of a person. You call this the pineal gland. It is a resonance that happens between animals and humans, the vibration of which actually physically affects the gland. Why is this relevant? Because that is the system in the human body that connects to the Web of Love, the Web of Life. Once that switch is on, all the animals can feel you. "Hear" you. Experience your essence. And whether you are consciously aware of it or not, it opens your world.

True unconditional Love will do this same thing, but in the glorious communion of All That Is, this is the perfect solution. For a humanity that is largely still unaware of their SoulMate, that has no identity as the great part of life they are, this Love shared with animals can mean everything. Thus, animals and humans have a great sacred interaction in this glorious Web. And, of course, the more consciously someone can open to the Love that is completely present and fulfilled in animals, the more benefit they will experience.

It is the intuitive understanding of this process and, of course, the timing of things, that are making what you call animal communication so important.

The Web of Life is a glorious song of gratitude for life. Every being who dances within and upon it is alive in rejoicing in his or her heart. As the joy goes forth, it is amplified. Then comes the harmonies, as being after being after being let their song of great Love pour forth. That pouring forth is a waving dance of energy that weaves together more and more and more Life. So the Web is vibrating in joy. This joy is created by the specific strains of gratitude and "charged" awareness of Being Alive–awareness of the unity, dancing, singing, swaying to a Song of Songs.

Now, to experience this explosion of Love in consciousness is the greatest joy. This pulsating vibrant light and color-washed web of moving energies is the experience of God, for the Love that is God permeates every atom. When I dance along these strands of Love, my being is swept and uplifted. I know within my being all the conscious lives that are present. There is, as God said to you last night, a boundary-less experience as energies are shared.

So in this I am cat, yet I am cat only in one corner of my consciousness. The rest of me is in this experience of communion with All That Is. Thus in my being does it sing the truth of God and all who are participants.

Out of this singing, dancing, glorious living energy of Love, (the very molten and flowing kind!) there are entryways into the world of slower vibration—what you would call the physical world. The "slowed down" or "congealed" Love. These entryways are points of consciousness where we can turn to "look out" into the physical world. All animals, all of us are more alive with more of our being in the moving, sparkling Web of Life than in the physical reality.

There is a flow of light through this Web that is the essence of the "light of Christ." It is the "golden" energy that some of you have experienced. This energy is a communication system throughout the Great Web. It is an "electromagnetic" energy and it delivers messages of consciousness throughout the Web of Life. This is the very same energy that is awakened in the human body when the pineal gland is activated. Once it is activated, through the experience of Love, then the human body is connected through this "gland" to the Web of Life. So when it is switched on, then you are able to experience the great and glorious flow of life. When this happens you become one of the "loops" on the Web of Life, and all the energies of life come dancing through you to be blessed and to deliver their blessings.

You then also become a completely "open circuit" for all of the connected consciousnesses to "travel through". Then you bless and grant a new awakening to the Web as you are added, as all is then blessing you.

So—a dog will hook you up. And—a cat will show you around. For as I said, the pure heart of unconditional Love is the essence of what all dogs are (and always remain unless mistreated or distorted in any way, usually by human interaction). Their Love will vibrate on your "pineal switch," and open the circuit of your being (physical and spiritual.) Once open, when the circuit of Love is flowing in its natural state in you, that is where we come in for we are the explorers. We always investigate every living thing. We investigate every movement of life, whether in form or out. Thus we very quickly learn the flow, the nuances, the voices, the currents of energy, the song of Creation. In this moment, this is how I'm leading you through this "message." Other times it will be different, but always it will be a song of gratitude.

Now that is the other subject. The entire experience of this flowing, light filled Web with being after being adding energy and blessing the Web with their own —it is gratitude that keeps the energy flowing. It is gratitude that keeps the Web of Life alive. Open. Vibrant.

I don't think you are managing to get this translated. It's all right. I'm just happy that you came to get me! There is one last little tidbit about this "circulatory system" of golden, flowing Love that you'll like. So, I'll see if I can get it through. There is a web or

91

system that is the natural world—all of life that is here on Earth, in or out of physical manifestation. There is a vast, vast Web that encompasses the All. Everything. It is the conscious SoulMates that connects the energies of the two. That is you.

I think you are going to need to sleep long and rebuild your energy before I can get this wisdom through to you. Don't be discouraged (never be discouraged!) This was a very important deepening of our communion. I am deeply gratified by your searching for me. Thank you!

*Many of Yael's communions with Magic take place while Magic sits on or near Yael's notebook. Many of the pages in her seventy-eight handwritten notebooks have blank areas with sketches that say things like "cat paw here" or "Magic Cat sat here." So much does she love them that Yael would never remove an animal from her presence, even when it is impeding her "work"!

We know the Creator
lives within our
every movement.
So not only can we
look around,
we can know
the answers
from the very movement
of our paw,
the twitching of
our tail!
The answers live us.

Observing How We Move
as Truth Lives Us

What are you waiting for? You are waiting for some mystical state in which you will know the answers that you seek. And, yes, you do have such experiences. And, yes you can feel the touch of Goddess upon your heart and God's light upon your face. But—here is my question to you. When will you realize that the answers are in everything?

I can bring you the answers that you seek, but not only I can. Everything can, for we all exist within the Creator. Every breath of wind, every leaf and twig, every cloud, every bird, every mountain does, and when you remember that you are also part of the Creator, you will know where to look. That is when you know every moment of every day will be a "conversation with God" through the glory of created life.

This is how it is in our world, for animals do not ever forget. We know the Creator lives within our every movement. So not only can we look around, we can know the answers from the very movement of our paw, the twitching of our tail! The answers live us. The TRUTH lives me. I am animated by the Love that is all and is streaming forth in me.

I want to show you how perfectly every single moment unfolds for a cat. I want you to see this because it is such a shame that human beings do not allow this life to sing them–do not allow the Creator to live them. As soon as you do, the Creator of All is all through you. Yes, by this I mean that every bit of God is shining though you. As your body. As your movement. As the way your voice sounds as it comes out from you! For not only do we live upon the Web of Life, the entire Web can be seen through each of us! You can look into my eyes and know the truth of any life, just as you can look upon a blade of grass or look within a butterfly and through them see the face of God, and feel the real and living touch of All That Is.

You are stretching for this information because it is foreign to your definition of things. You believe (I speak after fourteen years of continual observation...) that there is always a higher state you must attain. A perfect thought, an empty mind, a cleansed soul. This is only because you have forgotten yourself. You have forgotten your place in the Web of Life. It is a place that only you can occupy. It is a place that assures you continual access to the glory and beauty of All That Is. The place that brings you everything in Creation. Right to you.

What does a cat do to know God? I will answer from experience. I sit a long time, listening to the humming life that is the Web, the body of the Creator, the living joy both manifest and un-manifest. Then, I get up. I move. I give my entire being. I acknowledge that I am the point where I am All That Is. ***And then I watch to*** *see what I do.*

By the very movement of my body in relationship to the Web of Life is the expression of God, our Creator, the glorious All That Is, expressing through me. As I watch carefully, as I experience the meaning of my movement, I understand. I understand my relationship to All That Is—by how I live forth each moment. That will sound like strange words to you but it is correct. For every moment, you certainly live forth God.

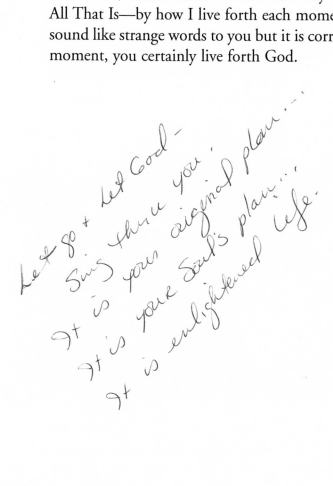

It's when you are
still and present
that you will
know God –
that you will
find yourself wrapped
in Her amazing Love
and awash
in the wonder of
All of Creation.

Being in Your Moments

At last! I have been sending you messages intently. Ever since the moment when reverence entered your life. This is where I come in! Because a cat is reverence for life! This is what I've been showing you. The All is right here. So glorious. So filled with light and beauty and satisfaction. I want to tell you that I know this reverence intimately. For while a dog may get excited about things and events, a cat simply is. Every moment we are in awe and reverence. Now I can begin to show this to you.

With every day you become more cat-like! This is very exciting. So now that you have begun, I get to take my real place as your teacher, and of course, your friend.

First, let me tell you about moments. When you watch a cat you can sense—even those people who have not yet come to this place of reverence—that the cat is looking deeply at each moment. You can tell that we are looking at things other than those you normally see. Well, all the time we seem to be dreamily staring out the window or off into space, we are looking at the Web of Life through the opening of each moment.

You cannot have reverence for life if you do not see it! And though you, and many other humans, grasp the concept of living in the Now, oh, you are not very good at it! Instead you are constantly flitting around, from past to future to past again–all of which exist only in the ever active synapses of your mind. Really and truly, until you can come to rest where you are, you simply won't be able to live in truth–what I see as Great Mother of All, what you term God. But not only this, you won't ever really be available for any of the glorious bounty that she ever pours on all Her blessed creations.

Reverence for life. It is the key to everything–and certainly the key to you. You can only have reverence if you are present. You can only be present Now. Reverence by its nature requires your ability to truly acknowledge that which you will revere. I am very excited! Because you at last will be here, meeting me in the glorious entryway to the sparkling Web of Life.

Come. Let me show you! See? Right here, with me, we are surrounded by endless beauty! In every direction you look all of it is present–for this is the whole of the Holy Now. Only when you love life are you able and willing to stop here and to simply be.

Humans have this incessant noise going on in their heads all the time. You should be a cat around a group of people (like the weddings in your wedding chapel). Ouch! It is enough to make any sensible cat run and hide (which we do!). The mind of a cat is open. There is no pushing from within us to be anything other than we are. Because life is so glorious! To be alive is the greatest, most magnificent gift! So each and every moment (as you count them) we are gazing in wonder at the glory of life.

Oh, yes, you know all of this. But have you lived it? You have not–not any of you. This is why Nature is the only hope for many people to find themselves an actual experience of life. That is what Nature is! And you, at last, are ready. You have finally gotten to life. You are at last free of that incessant chatter and the obsessive pushing which I understand is ego. See? You grasped it right away, now. Because you have an opening at last! This ego of yours wants to keep you out of the moment. It's when you are still and present that you will know God–that you will find yourself wrapped in Her amazing Love and awash in the wonder of All of Creation. For just as you've begun to see, everything is rainbows of light. Not a utopian and impossible dream cooked up by human longing. It's the absolute truth of Her splendor, lighting up Creation in all those trillions of ways.

See–you are doing it! You are having an agenda. You are creating a future. You have slipped into that mind again. And every single time you do you have slipped into the separation - this fancy show of no substance that is the chattering human ego. And every time it then succeeds in separating you from life, from the possibility of reverence, from the experience of the Web of Life, which can only be experienced Now.

None of you is living life You are not. I hope you will come to see this. I hope that you will listen to cats, Nature, all those who are truly present as the beauty of who She is and thus able to then experience yourselves!

I have to stress to you that only very lately have you begun to come into the actual experience of your life. All the rest of the time, when not in meditation, you have been living in your ego-built reality–completely disconnected from the real Love you are. I can't stress this enough! I know this is less the "dancing cat" tone I usually have, but this is SO important.

Even gratitude can be an experience of the mind (though I am now seeing how it connects you to Love's flow). Reverence can only be an experience of the Now. Standing on the Web of Life, actually experiencing all the glorious beings who share this precious universe, all the dancing light and glory, all the sheets of shimmering Love as it washes over everything. Oh–you are arriving! Arriving here where I can really share with you. Arriving where all life can come forth to show you its essence, its beauty, the specific and sacred pattern each life form is.

You have known you can communicate with the entire Web. With every single form of life. And you have had a successful beginning because even while your ego has had the upper hand, you have, with great determination, maintained connection with your heart. Now you are coming home to the great swirling whirling shimmering twinkling patterns of Love that are here manifested (some of them) as form. Coming home to the Now experience of their being.

When you have come at last to truly cherish life, then life will cherish you in turn. You have such great awareness, so much light, yet you have until now remained slightly detached. Somehow deeming this dense and real and solid, warm-blooded experience "beneath you." Finally you have realized it is all the same–that to cherish life is to honor the Creator and thus to bring forth the truth out of the swirling mists of the mind-stuff of humanity.

I can tell you that the doorway to the beautiful world of Love you hold so tenderly within you can only be accessed Now. Through this access, all is yours! All the magnificence of All She Is, right here. I watch, and into this space of watching comes such a flood of Love that I become a singing symphony of joy. I become the universes of Love within this body dancing in complete jubilation with the grand universes within Her, the great glory of Love.

First you must listen
to the breathing song.
As you listen
to the song of your breath
(even though you do not
have the ability to purr),
pay attention.
Soon you will hear
the harmony behind
your breath.
You will hear the
breathing songs of all
who share the Web of Life.

The World of Love is Right Here Where We Are

Asking the Animals to Assist Us

I want to tell you about the perfect world–about how the New World of beauty and perfection and Love can live right here in the midst of the old world. You know that I am an ambassador for the animals. I come to tell you that we have never left the perfect world. The world that we live in is right here in the midst of yours. And yet it is as different as the night is from the day. But there are those who can cross from world to world and we can tell you this–they exist in the same place. The world of perfection and the world of pain occupy the same space, share the same moon, breathe the same breath. Yet one world is heaven. The other…well…

An animal lives in the arms of God. We take our nourishment from the Mother–for while we cherish our physical food, it is the food of our heart that keeps us connected. We are woven into the body of life and we know that we are not separate from it. Thus every movement is sacred. Every breath is God breathing. Every motion, every lick and every sigh is the orchestration of a grand dance–a dance in which we know ourselves as the grand dancer and we know ourselves as the movement.

We watch. In our world we sit in communion with the world. The sky lifts us in visions. The wind sings lullabies, and we are suspended in a peace so deep that to move within it is to understand the nature of eternity.

Yet right beside us we see the other. It comes to us as a discordant symphony of random noises and movements that do not have the harmony. It is the dance without the dancer, for humanity does not know itself.

You can live here in the sacred world with us. To do so all you have to do is acknowledge the sacred moment –the moment where you enter into your contact with the Web of Life. It is the moment when you see the shimmering web and, touching it, are touched in turn by the glory and the beauty of the union of Love moving as form into the world.

We live in the sacred dance on the Web of Life each and every day. We do not forget. How you perceive us as outer beings has little to do with our experience. But we stand ready to lead the way. We stand ready to begin to show the humans who embrace us how to live in the Web of Life.

This is what you are referring to as living in the New World. But it is not new. It is as old as Creation. You have simply forgotten. So our good news to you is this–the animals can teach you. The bad news is that few will believe this. But we have come to understand that you are meant to be here with us–here being in this glorious trust of life. Here you can see the perfection of all life. You can see the communion of spirit that links all things, the Creator in whom we share this Web of Life. We have also come to understand that it is important for you to realize that the New World for which you are reaching is right here in the old one. It is simply an open heart away.

First you must listen to the breathing song. As you listen to the song of your breath (even though you do not have the ability to purr), pay attention. Soon you will hear the harmony behind your breath. You will hear the breathing songs of all who share the Web of Life. It will rise and then wrap you and carry you away through the vibrational doorway to the Real world of Love. This is the world in which we animals have our consciousness. When you can hear the song of all the teeming and glorious life in the world lilting around and through you, open your heart and open your eyes. There we will be! We will be sharing the New World with you in exactly the same space as the old world! But oh, how different it looks!

In this new experience of reality you can see the hearts of all beings. Each heart sings out Love (or not, unfortunately). The Love coming forth from each heart is like a bath of sunlight. You know how it feels when you lay in a puddle of sunlight on a cool day? It is just like this. It is wonderful. And it colors the area, too. As does everything.

Our world is filled with the colors of life, the sounds of life and the Love. These things are tangible to us. We acknowledge them all appropriately. Sometimes we rush to bathe in Love. Other times we just sit and sit and sit, listening to the song of the breath of life everywhere around us.

In our world we are surrounded by all the beings you cannot see–all of our animal friends currently visiting in their night-time bodies (when their physical form is sleeping) plus those not currently using a dense physical body. We also see those beings easily whom you call angels. Not to mention the lovely energies of spirits of Nature.

The reason I am explaining this to you is that I have come to realize, as your ambassador, that you need to understand my reality, because this is where you are heading. This is the same space that you occupy. The very same. But it is more alive, more beautiful, more awake than any of you currently dream. It is into this lighter reality that you are currently stepping. Please allow us to assist.

You humans have had many interesting relationships with animals, including a gathering awareness that we can and do communicate with you (continually!). But you would not think of us as spiritual guides for you, because you are very eccentric, thinking you are the top of the pyramid of Nature. But here is a bigger picture. We do not ever leave God's presence, because we are God's beloved creation expressing perfectly. We are not on an evolutionary journey. We are simply being, in perfection, what our Creator made us to be. I am Cat. I am gloriously feline, proud in my grace of being Cat as God made me. I walk this perfection with every step. I breathe it with every breath. And as I told you before, I know exactly where I fit on the Web of Life.

This does not mean that animals don't learn. We do. But we are not changing forms as humans are. We will be ever more Cat. So we do not forget, fall asleep, or have a part of us that dims the great light that we see ever shining within and around us. This is true for all of Nature. There is an element of behavioral reaction that can develop into an aberrant response if we are mistreated. But even then we still see the rest of the world. A dog that has been beaten will cower under the bed. But while he is under there he is communing with his circle of guides and friends who continually show him the truth. Thus our Love can be pure and straight and true even when our reactions might be molded by human mistreatment or other negativity

As an example, when I came to you (and, oh yes, I came straight to you because I heard your call), I was very hungry after the journey. But even while my body and senses developed an attachment to food as a result, at the same time I always knew that Our Mother held me in her arms. I knew that if I did not get food I would step out of my body and I would still be alert and comfortable in Her Love, for it is clear to me always that I am not this particular body. So while my body mewed and pictured food, I pranced and played on my way to you.

If you could gain this awareness it would be helpful to you, especially now because the body really does have its own intelligence. It has a separate consciousness. When you identify with it, as you do, it confuses you greatly. Yes, there is a point where a human being transforms out of a body/spirit and takes the body up as spirit, but I am not wise in those things. I only know what Cat wisdom provides me.

So when you worry about my leaving you, I want to tell you now that I know I am not my body. I can step out of this body with complete consciousness and continue on my way.

I would like to assist you to have this experience also. Not that you are leaving your body, but so you can tell the difference. The fear that you have been feeling has been coming to you from the larger "ball" of humanity. It is basically physical body consciousness and it is a rolling cloud of "fear of death." Evidently something is causing this to pour forth from humanity in huge eruptions. Whew. When I see it coming I want to hide! Then I see you suffer through it with grace, having little consciousness of what it is. Perhaps I can assist with some of these things. For often when you reach forth to God, you go up to the light to the "throne of God" to worship and commune. And this brings you many lovely things but not some of the more basic information such as acts of existence that I can explain.

As we continue our relationship you will find confirmation coming to you of things I will explain. You will understand why God has asked that I be the ambassador from the animal kingdom. It is because only true communion exists at this level of reality that you are seeing as the New World. Yet it really is the only world.

It is the world of Love as God made it. It is the world which humans originally occupied–a world of respect and joy and awareness and communion. So I will show it to you again. You have had glimpses, but I am going to take the shades off your eyes, the plugs out of your ears, and span the distance that seems to separate us, for as you are opening your heart, only thus will your experience of truth be complete.

It is all right here. It has never gone anywhere, this experience of your perfect world at this level. There is only beauty. All species still exist whose bodies have become extinct in the lower vibration level of the world. How can I explain this? Human belief, thought and feeling create an atmosphere. In this latest period of human history, this atmosphere has become too dense to accommodate the level of life needed by some species or beings. Plus the specific behavior and beliefs of humans toward those specific beings affect them directly, essentially denying their right to exist. This lack of respect of a being's life or a species' life truly sucks the life force right out of their physical body. This happens to humans also. So these beings or species whose life is not respected cannot absorb enough life force for their bodies, either individually or collectively, because they are covered over in human negativity. Oh, if you knew even a portion of the effect of thought and belief, not to mention action, you would really be shocked.

These species that have been essentially suffocated out of existence physically just step out of physical incarnation. But at a higher level they are right here. So as you come to live in this lighter atmosphere at the level of your Love, seeing through the heart as God has expressed it, you will find all of your beloved friends right here.

In the new world everything is nourished freely by God's Love. Since this level is moving energy at least at the vibration of Love, then anyone experiencing this world will see how Love manifests the world. Oh, what a difference there is. Even in your life you have seen what a shift from ego to heart can mean. Imagine if only Love exists! It does! Right here in the same space, just a few vibrations up.

This is what I am planning to show you. That you do not have to do anything but move into Love and your whole reality will change. First individually. Then collectively. For as God has explained for a number of years, there is no obvious path from where you are to where you are going. It's a leap into Love, which is the real truth of everything.

Oh, my human friends, how shall I show you the wonders that are waiting? Look into your Cat's eyes. Open your heart as you do so. They can take you through that moment into direct contact with the beautiful Web of Life. The Web is where all things are in Love. Perfectly.

Cats are very wise. Remember we do not have an ego. We simply ARE. We fully and completely ARE. As God made us. As is all of the natural world. Humming the song, alive with life. Feeling Love every moment, directly. Ready to share this experience with you.

We are ready–ready to return to right relationship with humanity. And you are ready too. You are ready to return to right relationship with the whole of natural life. Life is the most magnificent of God's attributes, the greatest of all the gifts of Creation. We need ambassadors like you just as you need an ambassador like me, because there are those in Nature who have withdrawn part of their energy. They have done as those who have become extinct and have pulled away from the lack of respect, the negativity, and so forth. But they are not gone yet.

So your outreach to them, showing forth genuine Love, will make a very big difference. It is not so much that you need to keep them here as it is that you must learn to honor all life. Until you do you will never be able to experience life as it really is. So you must practice loving so much, honoring life so purely that Love becomes your only reality. Thus if you are able to bring these parts of Nature back into full, present, participatory existence in this vibration, you will know you are successful at living in Love.

As Love is called forth as the reality, it will lift and cleanse everyone. You have communed with God about transformation. All that has to be done is make room for Love to become the one reality. Thus I recommend that you not focus on this process of cleansing or transforming. Instead just know that it will be the natural result of your continual choice for Love.

I am a very lucky Cat. (Lucky is not the word. Blessed is the word.) Here at Circle of Light there is little difference between my outer world where I live in my physical body and my inner world, where I am in communion with the real world. The Earth as it is meant to be. This makes for a lovely life. Many other animals admire this situation, for most who are in bodies are far less fortunate.

Cats have a good connection with truth in general, so it is easier for us in general than it is for others (especially dogs). Because of our nature, we do not take on the vibration of our humans very much (people consider this being independent). Dogs become very immersed. Yet they do also carry such a gift of Love to humanity that most often that Love will swiftly elevate the human situation. Most of the time it does, but sometimes it can take a few incarnations with their people to accomplish a change in the humans.

There is nowhere to go. There is only Love to be. Then that Love will tune in the New World and it will become your reality. Loving an animal is a fabulous place to start to make entry into the Real Home of all of us. Then, remember how it feels when you are loving the animal and decide to feel that Love for everything. Before you know it, the world around you will be changing dramatically as the energy of Love draws more Love to you. In Love all expresses perfectly. So there you have it! It is an entry into the full awareness of the world as God intended it.

Now, since like attracts like, once you are living in the world of Love surrounded by all the perfection that Love is, you can turn back and pour Love into the "milk bowls" of others! As you do and they drink it (okay–absorb it–but wasn't that a nice picture? A big bowl of milk? How about cream?) Anyway, as they absorb it, as long as you can get it into them, somehow that Love will begin to raise up their world. Before you know it, good things will be drawn into their lives by the Love you poured in. Before you know it, they will begin hearing the song. This is especially effective if you can really bathe them in Love (the only kind of bath a cat likes!). You can do this by delivering it personally (a very good plan) or with the help of their animals (if they have any). I say this especially to you because you never even think to ask for our assistance, but we are Love delivery systems. Pure straightforward and functioning beautifully. And we are eager to help.

It is most definitely time to step up the dialogue with us and with Nature. Please! It is time to leap forward. I am asking you to go from talking to us about peeing outside the box to engaging us in important things. We are completely connected to God. We live every moment in full awareness. As humans have discovered through experiences with marine life, animals have deep messages for humanity. All of us.

First we are a word of God. Each animal and every part of Nature has an essential meaning. So when a message needs to be delivered to you (when you are connected through your heart), an animal is sent to appear before you. When you understand the message of that animal in God's language then you know exactly what God, or your angel, is telling you. We love this service, for it is built into us.

Secondly, because we are ever connected to the truth, to the level of real connection of unity, all you need to do to utilize our assistance is send us your heart's desire and we will assist you. Nothing lower than the heart's desire will be accepted though. To set the record straight, we do work with those who are in communion with the world and who bless it by their magic. We do not work with those who are working "dark magic" or wishing someone harm unless we are actually overtaken by mesmerism—which happens very rarely because we are so connected.

We honor life. We love our Creator and all the amazing ways that the Creator's Love manifests. We always serve that Love, so if you serve it also we are eager to assist you. And we can show you many wonderful things—about Love, about life, about companionship and sharing and, very importantly, about bridging all gaps through Love. Love is the language that all Creation speaks. Will you try it? You just might be surprised.

I am so glad you are finally "studying" with me. How I love you! I love you every bit as much as you love me. I am going to guide you outward into your place as communicator, connector of all Life. Please place no judgment on our communications (such as God is most important/more important and therefore you should be talking with God first) because there is an opening for my assistance that I have been longing to fill. You might be surprised once the word spreads, especially with the young people.

Yael's notes in the margin of her meditation notebook on this day read: "Magic was insistent that he wanted to tell this information, this story, as he called it. He came and sat on the page, on my hand, and would not leave. I wrote. Magic was on top of me the whole time. In fact, he sat on my hand again and again. It was very important to him. He was most definitely a cat with a mission tonight. There was such Love and such a solid communion. He kept showing me that people were going to be open to this because he was telling it. How I love working with him!"

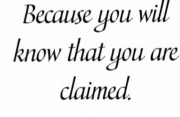

I ask you to
request the experience
of the Love.
Ask to know it,
in every fiber
of your being.
As soon as you do,
you will not ever
lose your way again.
Because you will
know that you are
claimed.

Humans Must Experience the Love

Today in my purring is the acknowledgment of the great and mysterious gift of the world, and how it shimmers in its special place within the Web of Life. For as I purr, I can feel the resonance responding as all of the Creation claims me as its own. It is often a topic of concern among the animals that human beings can see themselves as so alone. We have pondered this, because it is unfathomable to us. We have come to understand what agony this is, so we have all agreed that we must help you re-establish yourselves in the grand and glorious community of life.

We are known. We are known and loved and completely enfolded in the many-layered warmth of the Earth, and the great weaving of the very essence of ourselves into the tapestry of Love that is the world. And then, even more grand, we are known by name, by heart, by the signature of our heartbeat as a part of the living universe. There is never a step I take that the very Earth does not caress me. With every paw that touches the ground, I can feel the warmth of Love rise up my leg and spread through my body.

With every breath that I breathe, I can taste God. As it comes into me, it enters with a message of Love.

Every breath resonates with my name and tenderly elevates my being. I am lifted, opened, and exultant. I leap into the air in rejoicing.

I want so much to show you my experience of life, because I know you can reclaim it. You can remember that everything you see is God–God holding you, warming you, lifting, inspiring, and leading. Words are so woefully inadequate! Can you please imagine this kind of Love? Can you "test the waters" of the awakening to the singing and glorious Web of Life that is woven carefully by God out of the threads of joy that create a life?

One life, one seemingly small cat, and every step I take is a surge of God's Love pouring into my feet. Love is then shown to me from every direction. From every side. On every face of life. I stretch and I feel the Earth soften and lighten beneath me. The exultation of my existence is sung forth and I feel it expanding, multiplying, and coming back to surround me with more and more consciousnesses, more and more voices, more and more light. It is so beautiful, so magnificent, that I simply must sit. I must sit down to absorb it, to allow the Web of Life to acknowledge me and to sing me as a Love song in the world.

I know it is difficult for you to explain these things that I am showing you, but I ask that we continue together to do our best to keep describing. It matters very much to me that human beings can join the experience of the living assurance of how we are loved, the assurance that is all of ours every moment.

Oh, how you are loved and how deeply you belong. You belong to God, to All That Is, and every bit of it adores you —as you are meant to adore every bit of life–all of it!

Now in this we have come to the true magnificence of Creation. Adoration. The perfection of the circle of Love that is made of giving and receiving. As I feel the entire glorious Web of Life acknowledge me, as I feel the warmth of Love enfold me and the exuberance of Love move through me, oh, my being rises in joy. My heart opens wide and my adoration pours forth in waves.

I step forth and Love washes through me and I open my heart in complete adoration of the grand perfection. I, in turn, become aware of all the "faces of life" before me that are a part of this beautiful life. In that moment, like a bolt of lightning, the Creator's perfect Love comes shooting through me! Rushing forth to wash with a mighty glow every being sharing the life of the world with me.

I am alive in a magnificent glory of living Love, completely known and completely supported. Can you sense this and feel it beginning to come through to you? Beginning to lift up the veil of forgetting under which you live?

You are the only ones who can forget that you are considered by all of Creation to be the most beautiful and precious of manifested life. Only you have found a way to use your heritage of co-creation to create an existence where you are not loved! Where you can ever be alone, abandoned or cut off at all from everything.

It is beyond my comprehension to consider such a life, or should I term it, existence? Yet I can see the hole in many human lives where, as a result of their beliefs, the humming, glorious, warm, vibrating waves of Love that flow toward that person go right through them. It is because they cannot claim it for their own, I guess. So while they are surrounded by the glowing pink cascades of Love, it does not warm or elevate them. It does not connect them to the Web, but rather goes on through to bring radiance and joy to another being in the great Web.

So perhaps, I wonder, when I see such things, perhaps those who think they are alone, could explore the Web as a cat does? Can I show you, lovely humans, that you can open your eyes and heart and mind to be the recipient of the great Love already pouring through us?

There is a terrible striving and a noise of great and urgent yearning that issues from human hearts. It is an awful sound, for it is not a sound of harmony but like a cat crying for food. Yet even when our bodies are hungry or frightened we are ever aware of the support of all life. This human yearning is far more disturbing.

Oh, humans who yowl in such loneliness–all Love is right here. In every form. In every energy. Pouring on you in golden threads from the moon. Singing to you from the leaves of the trees, blessing you with the gentle and lovely movements of the butterfly. Love is ready to fill you with the experience of yourselves as Love that Love can live in the world in you.

Thus I ask that you take moments as I do to absorb the Love and to hear the song—to compose the poetry of each moment. And of course to show you everything is Love, prepared by the Creator in a million ways so you can thus see yourself as Love again and again and again, until it is fully absorbed into your consciousness. Until you agree with the Love and sing it onward in adoration to the rest of life.

You see, each moment a different form comes into your consciousness just so you can adore it. Oh, yes. And as you do, as you stop to behold its wonder, then you are in right relationship with the Web of Life. For just like breathing, or blood moving, we are the Love of Creation nourishing life with Love. So the Love must keep flowing. We are each required to do this. For if we don't, then the Love stops flowing through us! And just as happens if a physical being loses the flow of blood, a spiritual being cannot exist without the refreshing and life-sustaining flow of Love. Unlike a physical vessel, a spiritual being does not "die," but rather stagnates, which in a sense is a spiritual death.

So to every one of you who can be in the sacred presence, who can feel the sanctity of the flow of Love, please observe. Observe how desolate are those who don't remember how greatly they are loved. It is God's message to you that such a remembrance, such reconnection to the giving and the receiving will completely heal all who accept it, because you are, like us, simply packages of Love! Vessels through which God can pour the flow of Love. As soon as the flow is re-established, the being, whoever or whatever it is that has forgotten, is then re-established in the connection–the flow.

If you will allow yourselves to experience each moment as does a cat, you will know how greatly the blessings of the Earth feed you. As out of the Earth grows food for your bodies and ours, so also does it contain food for your heart. I ask you to request the experience of the Love. Ask to know it, in every fiber of your being. As soon as you do, you will not ever lose your way again. Because you will know that you are claimed. You are loved so much by so many that any second without your presence would be too difficult to contemplate. Knowing this Love is for you, you will also know this Love is you, and you will thus give yourselves permission to live only in Love.

You must choose to erase all the shadows that have fallen across your hearts and minds by simply facing the "sun," the source of real Love. Thus is the Web experienced and nourished. Thus is it returned to perfection. Every single moment you can look around you and see the evidence of Love everywhere. Accept the evidence, and the truth of the Creator's Love for you will be made manifest.

Stretch out a paw and feel the Love pulse through it. Breathe in the sweet air and feel it affirm all Love within you. Then step up and claim the Love that you are–that All That Is reaches forth in you for others, and in others for you.

An Album of Magic Cat

*Here is Magic in his early years—
a handsome young dude with
a mind of his own.*

Magic has always been an astute observer–especially when wedding guests are arriving.

Magic Cat and Christos enjoying the Web of Life.

Magic Cat before the Divine Feminine Fountain (any fish in there?)

Magic with his beloved mistress, Yael

Everyone knows the Message notebook is my favorite place

Why don't you listen to me more often?

Yael, no more writing today

Portrait of greatness

"I'm here!" Magic Cat returns in his new, pampered, pedigreed, Rag Doll body (on right) with his SoulMate, Magic's Love. (September 2003)

The "kitty apartment" with Love on top, Magic in the middle, and their sister Sweetheart on the bottom

Magic strikes a dramatic pose at 4 or 5 months with our friend Carrie

We're seeing "the old Magic" in this handsome, growing guy

*Magic Cat (above) with
his beautiful Love (below)
at about nine months*

The Master, October 2004

We are aware fully of
the Great Creator.
We breathe in that consciousness
as a backdrop to all life.
Then we also grant
the Mother and the Father
dominion in our life.
We move, breathe, eat
and sleep in the rich
enfoldment of the Mother
in glorious communion with
manifested life here on Earth,
and we worship the
great force of Love
that penetrates each of us with
that great ray of Love, as
the Father of all life.

The Difference Between Cats Hunting and Humans Eating Meat

Living in Harmony or in Fear

I am indignant! Oh yes, I definitely understood what you just read–and in a book supposedly by an ascended master! You read (unbelievably!) that animals did not exist until humanity "fell." It implies that we are some lower life form that came to be as a result of humankind's animal nature. Oh, let me tell you, this is the most ridiculous and human ego-centric thing I have ever heard! So, to set the record straight, first I must tell you that I am presently surrounded by animals in their spirit consciousness, all anxiously assisting me in giving you this information. It is definitely time for humanity to see that there is a different point of view than theirs. And it is time, way past time, for humankind to expand their perception of life.

We live in God. We are a loving outpouring of the Creator's delight. That is what animals are! Not, I repeat, NOT less than humanity! Different, yes. Yet in terms of how humankind is today, we are closer to God. We are living true to our nature. And, as even God has brought into your consciousness, we are each a sentence in God's language of life. Thus, how we interact in the world and with humanity, speaks. Every animal is a strand on the Web of Life, or you could also say a sentence in the mouth of God. Thus, any being, human or otherwise, who is really listening, knows what life speaks to him or her by our presence.

Everything is a part of the wholeness of life. Thus, for us and for all other natural beings, in every moment we are in holy communion with the Web of Life. Thus, if I see another animal, I hear the entire story of that moment. If it is a chipmunk that appears to me, here is how I listen, how I watch–how I know what our creator speaks unto me that moment.

First, I allow my senses to open. I note the smells. I feel the wind. I hear the birds. So I can understand who adds to this message. Then I see that the chipmunk is in a patch of sunlight. It is, as usual, difficult to put this in human terms. I read every part of the whole Web at the moment. Then we speak. I greet the chipmunk. I acknowledge the whole song. I breathe out and my breath spreads upon the ethers in greeting and acknowledgment. My breath then wraps around the breath song of all the others there in that moment's encounter.

Next, we dance and we sing together. Different dances happen, it is not always the same. On one day the wind and the sun and the chipmunk together might say to me, "Jump, chase!" Sometimes in that moment, the Mother says to me, "Take, eat, this is my body, that I now give to you, that you be lifted in exaltation into the joy of life." And then I jump upon the chipmunk, knowing that everything in the song is in harmony

Other times the Web hums to me, "Admire him, this chipmunk, for he exists for the Mother and he must live a little longer." I bow my head in acknowledgment. I still might prance, hold out my paw, show the little guy what a perfect hunter cat I am, but that day he will "get away from me." Of course, he doesn't get away. It was not right in the heart of life that I eat him that day. And so I don't.

Now I ask you, is this a being who is "less than" a human? No! So I show you this so you can see that until humans are part of the conscious Web, no matter how "cosmic" the message, it is only their own heart speaking. I can tell you what happened with that "ascended master" message you were reading. Exactly what has happened to everything. That man has become disconnected from the Mother. He only knew the Father's energy (and distorted, at that!). He was writing that earlier in this time (century) when the ameliorating energies of Mother Love had not yet been felt. So he could look up, but not out and down.

Oh, please, please, please, pray daily that such lopsided energy quickly be balanced, for your world is still tilting crazily with this disconnected masculine energy. You also noticed that he also railed against sexuality, exclaiming that it must be raised up, put away, transformed, or you will become old and decrepit and basically rot away. Now, because you think it is a "master" speaking, you doubted your truth. Since I am your special cat, I must set you straight.

The Father should not ever be worshiped without the Mother! Oh, what a disaster it has been that humanity has done this. *That* is the problem. Then anything that was life-giving became blasphemous, sinful (awful concept, yuk!). Including animals. Women were burned. Animals killed by the millions. Ugh! What a nasty part of human history.

I want to quickly get my attention out of that smelly and awful place, but I do have one more thing to say. I just mentioned the millions of animals killed because humanity has forgotten the feminine, the mother, the Web of Life. This brings me to eating meat. I do want to add my perspective since I am, after all, ambassador for the animals.

Only if you can honor the Web should you ever kill animals to eat. To rip someone's life away without honoring their spirit, without listening to the song and the dance, is not right. Now you humans look at cats and you say, "How cruel. They torture their prey; they play with it before they ever kill it." Yes. But with every swipe of my paw, I place my heart in their service. I say to them, "I salute you, lovely chipmunk. May you dance upon the Web tonight. May you visit me in my dreams and tell me of your journey." And as he leaves his body, I say, "Great Mother, to you I give myself and I offer you this life. Please take him to your starry breast and give him a journey worthy of him."

All of this I sing. You can even hear the song, if you listen, while a cat is stalking their prey. Little noises escape our throat, for we are singing in the ecstasy of the dance. We are, in that moment, purely cat, totally as our Creator made us. In alignment with The All. We know that the wind's song and the great movement of life are on course, and we are on course in it.

Never would we herd great groups of animals to slaughter and callously watch as they are frozen in terror. Oh, never would we kill anything without great respect for the beauty of its being and how great a gift the Mother gives. And never would we watch life ebb and turn a cold heart upon the scene. Never. For we know that life will honor us when it is our time to leave. We know that all around us will be the spirits of those we have killed. And we know that we can trust them to hand us carefully across the divide, just as we did them.

Would you place your crossing in the hands of those whose bodies you have eaten? Oh, I don't think you would want to! And if you would not, then you have not lived rightly. Think upon this. Being a cat, I have no judgment about the eating of meat, although I believe it is not the correct food for humanity. But regardless of that, I know that in terms of relation with the holy Web of Life, humanity should cease eating meat immediately until the treatment of and attitude toward animals is changed completely .

Now, I do understand that with meat in your system you have more energy. But you, more than anyone, should never eat an animal killed in such a horrible way as the meat you bring home. Oh—I like it when you eat meat because I love it. But I don't like the energy. Have you wondered why your cats always have preferred seafood cat food? This is the answer. We are very sensitive animals, being in a position like this where we are going to be communicating. And we do not like the energy that is in those cans of cows and pigs and turkeys! Because those are the by-products of the meat you are eating. And it is terrifying.

I hope all of you will listen to this. Those cans are basically processed fear. So is the meat you humans eat normally. It is very important, if humanity is to join us in the raising up of humanity and human inclusion in the song of Life, that you not take such fear into you. Not into your bodies. Not into your minds. I can promise you, that is not life.

I have, of course, "gotten" everything that flows through your consciousness. So I understand that you are grasping the importance of choosing Love and not fear. I also have "gotten" that you are completely unconscious about these ways that you feed yourself fear continually. Well, let me tell you, I would much rather—oh, there is no comparison—be killed by a cat like me than by a human in a factory.

All animals know about the horrible cruelty of such places—and such places are everywhere. As long as such places exist, there is a gap between humanity and animals that cannot be bridged. Thus I ask all who can understand this to become champions of animals whose fate is such a horrible death. And please do not put their death into your body (or ours). If there is some reason that you need to eat meat, then it is imperative that you find a respectfully killed animal for your source. There are so many reasons for this—to honor your own body, to gain real spiritual awakening. Also to not have fear filling you up inside! To be honored by the Web of Life and that may be the most important of all, for unless such honor is afforded you, you will not have a fully harmonious life.

Now I see this thing in your mind saying that such meat is too expensive. Oh, you better watch out if you don't want a "cat tirade"! (Remember that "righteous anger" of Jesus? Oh yes, we know him well.) It is far too expensive not to change. Expensive in health. Expensive in spirit. Expensive in respect. And expensive in fear–the very thing you must conquer if you are to enter into the communion of the Holy Mother's Web of Life! I think you have such a very warped value system! My cat advice? Either accept what you consider expensive (note that when you are in the Web of Life, all of life will be taking care of you), or stop eating meat. Even you could find other solutions, like eggs.

So–this, I do believe, qualifies as "Cat Lecture Number One." However, as you can see, I have a very big responsibility, being in this position as a "spokesanimal" for all of the beautifully connected members of life on Earth. We do want humanity to join us in the conscious worship and joy and Love that is right relations to all of life. Humanity is different from the animals. You have a great heritage, which most of us trust you will one day fulfill. And we are in communion with the Masters of Light which, luckily, assure us that there is hope for humanity.

There are some animals who want nothing to do with humanity. However, even those will come forth to speak God's language to you if God asks them to. For animals are motivated—no that is not the word. We ARE. We are the perfect expression of what God made us to be. Thus, we will always obey God's Will.

We do recognize the forces of Creation. We are aware fully of the Great Creator. We breathe in that consciousness as a backdrop to all life. Then we also grant the Mother and the Father dominion in our life. We move, breathe, eat and sleep in the rich enfoldment of the Mother in glorious communion with manifested life here on Earth, and we worship the great force of Love that penetrates each of us with that great ray of Love, as the Father of all life. And we know absolutely, totally, unfailingly, exactly how they go together to be life and to sustain together this blessed Creation.

You will learn these things. I will happily teach you. I can explain with my every breath and my every movement just how perfectly they dance together, pouring out their Love into being as us and supporting us within themselves always.

You are an energy just like them, except greatly diminished in force. So we do acknowledge your promise, at the heart of your being. The Mother and the Father both tell us to wait patiently and we will witness a miracle as humanity is born back into the Web. We shall see.

I'm available to assist. I am a very important cat, coming forth just to be here with you at this time. I am so glad you are finally listening. I have been waiting, but you had to grow to an entry point before we could begin. Now our great Love will bring good into form. And I too love our new closeness.

To all who are listening, I give my regards. It is true that I am a very lovely, unique and "cool" cat. And Yael, I am always your Magic Cat.

With no "might"
or zest or true delight,
you can't put any
"oomph"
behind your creations,
or your reaching for
experience of union.
With God/Goddess or SoulMate,
everything is energy.
Everything.
So please practice
running your energy
through your whole beings —
all the way up to the heavens
and down to the
heart of the Earth.

The Ecstasy of Union with God/Goddess

"I greet you as the presence of God/Goddess, our Beloved Creator. What joy can we share together in this moment?"

This is how those in the natural world introduce themselves. This is my greeting to everything and anything that I meet. If I am on the deck and a fly comes into my field, I stop. I hold very still. And I sense that fly with my entire being. I sit within the space of our meeting and I honor the fly. In the moment of our meeting there is nothing else. There is only the acknowledgment of life. Life meeting life. God meeting God.

We speak then, in the languages of energy. I marvel at the movement of its wings. I hear the little engine of its heart. I note the direction of its intent. Then I am expanded. The energy pulsing around our meeting, which is a warmth and a buzzing of vibration, expands. I take in the larger deck, the other insects, the trees and sky, and the many nuances of this meeting of Goddess. This then grows into an awareness of being cradled in the Great Presence. Then our meeting is complete, for in that larger framework I experience it. I experience the wholeness of our meeting. I acknowledge God before me and Goddess within me. I see if there is a larger message for me in Goddess' language as fly. Whether there is a direct message or not, there is always a meaning—a meaning as the weavings of Love softly join and caress and then join again in another way.

Then I turn my head. The experience shifts. If there is no life form in my view with which to commune, then I become enamored of the larger patterning—the energies swirling above that you would call angels—the beautiful, oh, so beautiful voices of the wind—the glorious touch of the sun. And every one responds to my acknowledgment. With every connection of my consciousness with another, a very real conversation will ensue.

And through every single one of these, Goddess shows myself to me. I am cat. I am cat grand and all powerful. I am cat, beautiful and decorative. I am cat, the angel's messenger, as I rise to come to you. I am cat, the serenaded, as the wind sings me Love songs. I am cat, the Magic one, as you look at me. And in each of these, I know myself in all my possibilities—for this is the blessing that Goddess gives us in this glorious universe. We are ever discovering. Discovering our Creator in all Her majesty. We are ever in Love with Her as we merge in passionate embrace with every form of life.

This is LoveMaking. Oh, I live a grand life of ecstasy! I live in the great LoveMaking of God (or Goddess, or whatever words describe them, the glorious positive and negative energies of All That Is). To us in the natural world, this is how it looks. If we are male, as I am, then Our Creator is She. And in every encounter with any other energy within Her being, I am merging with Her.

With every being and every energy I encounter, I am joined in ecstatic holy embrace. I move forth in openness and I am absorbed into each and every part of Her. I am merged in my being in a beautiful melding of heart and spirit. In this joining, I experience completely who this being is in Goddess, while we are joined in a passionate embrace of spirit. Thus I know that being, be it fly or mouse or butterfly–I have become one with it.

I know this must be the same experience that you humans have Making Love with your SoulMate. It is a complete melding of being in which I am one with them. In this moment of oneness, my consciousness expands to take in the whole of Creation as it relates to the union I am experiencing. This moment is pure bliss. "Ecstasy," I believe is what you might call it. This joining is a thrust and an acceptance, just as in the physical act of sexual union. And it is experienced with 100% of my entire being–my body, my cells, atoms, rivers of blood, sparkling nerve fibers, flashing twinkling lights of expression and feeling.

This becomes expanded into the explosion of Creation. So you see, I am Making Love with God. Or, actually I guess I should say, I am Making Love with Goddess, because when the Creator takes me into each experience, it is what you would call sexual, for Creation itself is ever pulsing with the original explosion of Creation.

I have observed carefully human orgasm in LoveMaking. And I got it! It is the exact same thing! The pulsing waves of ecstasy and feeling that humans have is the very same thing that is happening eternally with Goddess. And the moment I "enter into" a communion with any form of life, I experience the same thing. The moment I allow myself to merge with Goddess, at that moment I experience the "waves" of ecstasy. There are pulsations that lift and thrill and bless every fiber and particle and energy of my being. I experience this always when I greet, in Goddess, another being or living energy. This is a LoveMaking. However, it seems to me that it could be just simply experienced with Goddess, rather than with Goddess as mouse or Goddess as tree or Goddess as wind. This I don't know because for me it is always as a communion with another entity.

The reason I am sharing this is to help you "get out of your skin." I want to assist you to go beyond your belief that orgasm is two people, and begin, together, to join the ongoing LoveMaking that is God/Goddess. I know that you, dear human friends, are on the verge of something very, very big, because you have a special relationship with God. So when you can leap that divide, "get out of your skin" in a sense, and join in this way of greeting and experiencing life, you will be universal citizens. You will also, at long last, finally begin to grasp the amazing, mind-boggling beauty of Nature and the gift of this world you live in.

We of the natural world have watched with disbelief your display of selfishness. But, ever loving, Goddess began to show us how to see you with compassion and Love. She showed me how limited your vision is and said to me, so gently, in that way of Hers,

"Magic, can you imagine living life like this?" This She said while showing me how most of you believe that everything you are is locked inside your bodies. No glorious permeability. No sense of singing wonder as you touch energies with your aura. No view of the scintillating wonder of living vibrations of light that we see everywhere. Well, I certainly found my eyes opened. (Here Magic began to softly bite my hand, which he rarely does. I felt he was saying "Pay Attention.")

I offered to help you all, on the spot. That is why we now communicate. I also have become a great advocate for humanity with all the spirits of Nature, explaining this discovery of your plight to others. It is so far from our reality that we would never even dream it could be that way–that limited. Consequently, there is a lot of distrust of humanity in Nature, since so much has been pillaged. However, it's being my experience that once I show others what Goddess showed me, that all are first shocked into silence, and then their outlook is changed. I would like to ask for your assistance–yours and all who are willing to make the effort. As I open as many doors as I can, I ask that those of you who are filled with Love make contact quickly so that the natural beings can actually see the potential for a "new human" emerging (as She also explained to me).

This outreach, by me and others we can recruit, followed by loving contact, I think can bring very dramatic change. And there is supposed to be a very beautiful synergistic relationship between humanity and Nature. Plus, as you know, the Earth itself is an expression of your collective beings, your "place in time and space." Bringing this forward into consciousness could be very important.

I know that I am a very specially-placed cat, being here at what I call "the communion center." And I also know that great good can and will come from our relationship. Every part of human reality has to now come under jurisdiction of God in you. Communication will become the enlightenment of the Holy Spirit. Meaning that you will understand the larger meaning of every encounter, especially, I hope, with your interaction with the natural world.

All of Nature is in Love. We exist right in the moment. And anything fully present in the moment is experiencing the Now of Creation. So as we move into this new joint venture, you'll have to remember to explain things to us. Explain how it looks to you as well as reaching with all your might for the real experience. And, since I said this, let me go ahead and add something. I said "with all your might." It is my/our observation that humans have no "might." No real zest, no strength of character. God has shown me the reason for this. All the above expressions are energy movement. Well, in order to move, there has to be room to build up momentum. If I start to run after something, the longer I run the faster I can go. Well, if humans believe that the parameters of your being are your physical vehicle, you have no room to get your energy moving. And the biggest motivating force is delight. Joy. Exhilaration. Well, as you know, because of your beliefs, humanity has very little true delight.

With no "might" or zest or true delight, you can't put any "oomph" behind your creations, or your reaching for experience of union. With God/Goddess or SoulMate, everything is energy. Everything. So please practice running your energy through your whole beings –all the way up to the heavens and down to the heart of the Earth. Decide on JOY. Decide to Make Love with life, with God. Because I can promise you, it takes outreach with "oomph" to connect with life.

Do not ever be fooled by our cool, fabulously composed presentation. We cats definitely have "oomph." We have might. We can leap from one thread of the Web of Life to another. We can play with the glorious, many-many-faceted faces of Goddess that are the expressions of the Creator's vast and gloriously playful, exuberant mind.

I am aware that you are also, as well as studying the ecstatic nature of All That Is, wanting to experience only the perfection of God/Goddess living as you in each moment. I honor this very much, for this is exactly the expression of animals.

Every animal is a "sentence" or symbol in Goddess' language. We each know that when we are sent forth, or moved by the spirit, to present ourselves somewhere, that Goddess is expressing as us. This is an even more profound experience. It is so because we can experience what/who we are in Goddess as we were perfectly created to be. And if the other person/animal/force or being gets the message, oh, there is an exhilarating communion of being that is the out-picturing of our perfection, because then we are delivering for Goddess. And this is the greatest reward. The deepest satisfaction. It's like a double experience of the waves of ecstasy.

There is the amazing NOW communion as our being makes the merge with the other, and there is Goddess pouring through us in joyful salutation to the being that we greet. And this is also waves of ecstasy again. So there is ecstasy rippling from us as we join the other and ecstasy pouring (with oomph!) through us to the other. Oh, boy, is this ever yummy on every level. Thus, as we now commune, every time this connection is made, I am delivering my message as Cat–Perfect Cat-ness - and you are receiving. This is another type of LoveMaking. This is the "inter-life form," God-directed communion that is so very important.

So if you can remember to allow God/Goddess to **deliver the message of you** as you greet another, you will have succeeded in what you are wanting to accomplish. For you want to be the hollow reed; to allow God to completely express through you. The one last step, though, that will make you successful is realizing that God/Goddess wants you in the equation. Not your little limited being, but you as Our Creator created you. For, like us, you also have a message to be delivered. But as God has explained to you, you can't quite see this yet (because you're focused on way too small an area).

This part is hard to explain to human beings (in comparison to animals) because you are something limited. Animals know they are not, so it's more obvious to us. So to be the hollow reed is not to be empty (at least not what you are wanting to do). *It is to be yourself with such passion and grandeur that you switch to the unlimited version of yourself and thus you see the unlimited version of whoever is in front of you!* And thus you see them as God sees them. As you know, like attracts like, so you will draw before you what you are able to experience. So you have to fully be you as God/Goddess sees you in order to see them as God/Goddess sees them. And then you will see and feel and know every bit of Our Creator's Love for them.

You will experience God/Goddess loving them through you. You will see and know just how passionately Goddess loves them. You will feel how every tiny hope of theirs for true Love or a better life is so exciting to God—how time means nothing because God/Goddess is so patient. If it takes years for a couple to break through to one moment of true Love, God will rejoice in that moment as much as when they were created. Every little forward movement is so precious to Goddess. And every person is loved as if they were God/Goddess' only child, as if every turn of their eyes or move of their hand is a spectacular blessing of Love for God. Yes, you and I, all of us, are so tenderly loved by Goddess that all of our good is being poured upon us. Oh, yes. Pressed upon us.

The difference is that I can feel this and you can't. Yet knowing what I do about the doors that need to open for humanity quickly, I know it is time for all of you to experience this Love. Isn't it truly miraculous? I'm realizing all the good that I need to share with you. The amazing explosion of the waves of Love as you meet/merge with others. The passion of really

155

acknowledging yourselves.   The glory of experiencing yourself as God knows you. Oh, that is so good. And as a result, the experience of how Goddess loves the being in front of you.   And on top of it all, the great blessing of every rainbow—a moment of overflowing good, delivered by God, pouring upon your head in an avalanche of blessings.

Oh, what a life. And to think, people see a cat and believe there is nothing going on. Human beings believe we are serenely sleeping all the time. SLEEPING! If I had ego, I might be offended. Oh, I can tell you, sleeping we are not. We cats are always awake to the glory of Goddess. Humming and vibrating and dancing within and dancing on the Web of Life every moment.

I have even more that I can share with you, but I think you'll find that this covers many of the things you wanted to explore. We are great partners. I'm glad you called for me, all those many years ago. Is it 15 now? Time is irrelevant, yet it does represent a long-term commitment to partnership. That number might tell people what a team we are, you and I. And we are just getting to the exciting part.

Come dance with me! Isn't this storm fabulous? It definitely has OOMPH!

The following notes were in the margin of Yael's notebook with this message: "WOW! Wonderful. What an amazing being Magic is. I forget how observant, astute and tuned in he is to what we are learning. This was SO good My Guru is a Cat!"

When you
open your heart
and go beyond your mind,
all that you experience
is yourself.
And the heart will only "see"
what is real.
Thus, when you proceed
to turn this open heart
to touch upon another human,
you will experience them
AS YOURSELF –
as God expressing Love
in yet another magnificent way.
And you will have only
pure and tender Love.

You Are God
God Is Everything
Breaking Free of Our "Loopy Mind"

First, let me tell you that I don't need to be here lying on the notebook for us to commune. Certainly, you know this. However, somehow it always makes you feel better if I am–like it's proof that we are communing. This is a concept that **must go**. The whole idea of space and distance is hypnosis. You have been mesmerized into believing that you are "here" and other things are "there."

Part of what I want to do today is give you a roving cat report. I want to feed to you, through your true perception, the truth of life as it hums, dances, blossoms and rejoices around you. I certainly want to expand your day-to-day reality, as you call it, into your eternal reality - NOW. This is what She has asked me to do, and I do it with delight!

If a cat could (or ever would) do something as undignified as jumping up and down to get your attention, that would have been me yesterday. I am SO glad you heard me. On Tuesday, when Our Creator was releasing you from your limiting perceptions, you were having trouble getting all of it. Right then I understood that I am to assist you and I had been wanting to get your attention ever since.

Do your best to see the world through my perception and I will do my best to cross the bridge, so to speak, into your linear reality.

As open as you are, you are not open enough. Because you still see God as "out there," and now you are moving into seeing God "in here," meaning within you. But here is the truth: God/Goddess is everything. Not "in" everything. IS everything! The Web of Life is a scintillating wholeness, every single moment of which is always expanding in a glorious explosion of Love. This is God/Goddess, our Creator. This is US. What God is asking of you in this time is the release of your boundaries and the jump into the One.

Can you see as I do? This twig is a shape of Her, our beloved God/Goddess, oh, every definition and beyond. Yet when I look upon this, I see a shape of the Goddess and a new and interesting expression of myself! I feel the shape of it within. I feel the movement of its life - its attachment to a large tree, its drop to the ground, and now its progress back to Earth, and this process then speaks to me. It speaks of the textures and movements of God and it speaks to me of me, of a new note in the song that is All. As I embrace this awareness, the whole of myself is expanded and I sing with God/Goddess, and as the Goddess, as this piece of Her expresses within me. Right here. In this moment of communion, all of that which you have labored to record IS, altogether, now.

Yes, it definitely came through to you intuitively in our first moment of communion far more easily than it is now. But let's keep going–because I know I can give this to you. To all of you. For life is JOY. Oh, it is joy upon joy upon amazing and glorious joy. And every bit is God revealing God to Herself. It is God as Herself expressing in motion. All directions, all at once.

I have often pondered why God speaks to you of the "New World" when everything spoken of is here. It is still a mystery to me, but I have had some glimpses as I touch into your mind. Wow! The convoluted barriers to the simple, direct experience of ongoing Love expression, which is the Creator AS all of us–it is stunning. How can I be of service in helping all of you slip beneath that linear thinking and back into the truth? I ponder this often when you are near me.

I ponder this often because when you approach you are in a "bubble of babble." You are ever talking to yourself. Describing this, evaluating that. Putting names and definitions, colors, and of course, evaluations of what you think. And this bubble keeps you looking at yourself all the time. All of you. So unlike all the rest of life, you human beings are the only ones who are living second-hand. You experience almost nothing directly. And I have figured out that it is this "intermediate self" that is ever feeding you reality. It is what creates time for you, because it separates you from experience and you then define your days and nights ever further. I see it but it is difficult to get through to you because we live so differently.

I am a very unique cat. Most animals have no interest in even getting their paws exposed to this big lake of separation, of time, and of all these millions of "bubbles of babble" that humans walk around within. But our relationship changes this because you are opening. You want so much to know, to understand and to love. And we have ever been companions (and ever will be), so I have "caught the fever." I, too, now actually ponder these things as I clean myself. Sitting in the grass and trees down below, I look up on this wonderful house and I see the rays of light pouring forth (just exactly as Our Creator has described) and I find myself thinking BIG. Beyond cat-ness. Into communion. You have also drawn around you a very large group of interested animals. These animals are also catching this desire to assist humanity. We all know that Our Creator is responsible for this urge. It swells up within Him/Her in Her desire to have you back. So we know that everything in existence will now be feeling this tender love and longing for humanity's freedom

Now—back to my discoveries. What God is moving you into is the awakening to the experience of yourself as everything, especially Nature at this moment. Nature is the perfect beginning for there is no separation —no distance between the being and the experience of itself as God. The experience of itself as God! This is where you are to look—all of you. Unwrap the bubble and open yourselves to life, naked of thinking without any definition of anything. Just thrust forward your heart. Open your eyes. And allow the recognition to begin. As you see the beautiful bird swooping through the air, allow only your heart to experience it. No thoughts. *Remember, this is what God calls the old world: the mind in between you and the experience.* You must now eliminate the mind. You may call it old mind or even lower mind, if you must, but it is exactly such definitions that keep you separate.`

Without your mind engaged at all, FEEL the experience through your heart. There will rise in you an exhilaration, a sense of freedom, of glory, of pure experience. This is how we live life–absolutely directly through/in/as the heart. And your hearts are as the center of Creation. So when you at last move into this–*you will understand (not mentally) that you are All That Is.* The resonance of joy, the communion of IS-ness, of bird and air and light and wind and your Love will show you who you are. You are that. You *are* that. For you are God, and God is everything. Not in some second-hand way. Directly.

This experience–the direct, glorious all–encompassing heart experience of oneness–is your New World. It is all you. It is all God, and God is the passionate explosion of Love. God IS LoveMaking! This experience, the experience that All That Is is always having in the Eternal Now, is like an intimate, tender, yet exhilarating and cosmic Love Affair. God, our Creator, is Love experiencing the expansion of itself.

When you Make Love physically, I can see you breaking out of the circular mind (that bubble I spoke of). I see you literally shooting up beyond it. So for a moment then, each of you can touch the Now. The ongoing moment of God's Love with nothing between you and the experience. What you are to have now is the awareness that everything you touch through your heart when you are beyond the mind IS YOU. IS GOD. IS LOVE. GOD LOVING GOD in trillions upon trillions of ways.

When you open your heart and go beyond your mind, all that you experience is yourself. And the heart will only "see" what is real. Thus, when you proceed to turn this open heart to touch upon another human, you will experience them AS YOURSELF–as God expressing Love in yet another magnificent way. And you will have only pure and tender Love.

But we are starting with Nature, for in its purity it is easy for you to see the perfection, the beauty, expressing there. This, then, is to be your practice ground until, perfected, you are holding yourself in Love every moment. Then we can move outward from there.

I am to teach you. Our Creator said to you, "Love Me through loving All Creation," and showed me that in this way you can know yourself. First, then, I have to tell you something. What you have perceived–all these beautiful Messages [from God] that lift you so high, that release you into a new experience of this tender, glorious, amazing Love–they DO NOT COME TO YOU THROUGH YOUR MIND! You are aware of the lifting, the light, the expansion. You are aware of placing words on them. The experience itself is the direct communion with the Love of God. This is why you must translate them.

Well, your next step, this new man and new woman you are becoming, is life in the heart only. There is a faculty of perception that is completely beyond "mind" at all. This is where we live. This is why your scientists cannot believe that animals communicate. They are looking at our brain. So they say, "Well, perhaps a dog can understand like a two-year-old; a cat lives on instinct, and birds, well they are only mimicking if they seem at all to communicate, because look at the size of their brain! Certainly they cannot think!"

What you call the "mind," well, it is as your idea of a bird! It is only a loop of mimicking, programmed responses that keep you away from the direct experience of life. Because of this, I will use the heart to describe real communication. In truth though, it is your entire being. When you open your "bubble," throw wide open your chest, your heart, you are also opening everything. The cells of your body receive this Love. The atomic structure of your being (far larger than your body) receives this communication. The living electrons - which is your real circulatory system that is linked to All That Is - every one receives the communication! The only thing that does not is the false "mind" that is a buffer zone keeping you from experiencing yourself.

Once you begin to have the experience, here is how it goes. You open the bubble and you throw open your being. You begin to see as I see. The shimmering, glimmering, twinkling, iridescent, magnificent, singing ecstasy fills you and lifts you. Oh, it is far beyond what you call your six senses. You can feel the exchange of Love circulating through you and out through the All of God.

You are a part of the living, loving being of God. Every part of you is fed, topped up with Love. You can tell you are "right with the world," so to speak.

In this experience, your eyes light upon a bird. Oh —words. HOW can we get this across for others? You are the buzzing, dancing light-filled, living piece of God, standing here, on our deck. You feel the "light blood" circulating through you in an exhilarating flow, bringing consciousness and joy to every single tiny particle. You look upon the bird. You are awed by the beauty. Look at the magnificence. Oh, precious little feathers, perfect beak, lively eyes! You feel the light begin circulating very brightly between you. This becomes the recognition that All is God. You are God loving yourself and loving yourself as bird. The more you love bird, the more you love you. You as you, you as bird. Together, standing in the eternal now of ecstatic, pulsating Love that swirls within and all around as ever more expressions of who you are.

You can sense the huge magnitude of your truth, the great cosmic nature of your being. Yet in this moment, there is only this Love. This treasured intimate amazement of bird, every single feeling of which floods you, rocks and lifts you, until your boundaries as bird and human completely dissolve and all the Love you were feeling for bird you recognize as your Love for God and you know this as yourself, as well.

It is these moments of knowing that bring you fully into your truth. Eventually you will stay like this. And you will be spiritual only. There will be no human mind in you. In this moment, you are free. This is what you name ascension. It is nothing more (or less) than becoming All and Loving All, and never taking back the smaller human mind.

Could you feel it? Because this real you–it is feeling. It is not thinking. It is the feeling nature of Our Beloved Creator that is the energy by which Love ever reaches for itself! The glorious being that you look to as your example (Jesus)–I have pondered him as well. You call it having the "mind of Christ," but I do not see any "mind" within him. The great and glorious intelligence of Creation, of God and Goddess in their glorious union, is LoveMaking. This will sound strange only because you don't understand the fact that Love is everything. It is not some things, but not the rest! So Love is the only real intelligence. Oh, it communicates perfectly. Love delivers its truth like a sweet, tender caress–like being rubbed and petted by everything. It is a voice that speaks very clearly inside each being. Oh, yes, every single one! Even those your little mind labels inanimate. They hear Her even more clearly, because they are still.

I know that human little minds will argue that mind is a universal thing. I stand firm. It is not. Has not God Herself/Himself said to you in every imaginable way (including every "holy book") that LOVE is all there is? "Case closed," as you say. Mind is a shadow dance, as you have called it. I can tell you this. Get rid of that mind you cherish so much and you are home free!

Now, before you have a "people fit," (instead of a cat fit!), let me remind you that this does not mean you lose intelligence. It means you graduate into *real* intelligence. And I can, by all I am (and I am an amazing cat!), swear to you that if you still that (horrid) little mind, if you get rid of thoughts, you will finally know everything. I can also swear that out of your heart will arise the whole truth. Instantly, fully, every moment, in the moment. You will then know everything. Everything you need (or want) to know, rising up to complete your experience of God. This means that you can know all God knows! You can open or "tune into" any thread of Love connected to your Now experience. Then, in the next moment, you can know the next fullness, the everything related to your current Now experience. So your knowing has no limits. Unlike your mental learning, you need never retain anything. For it is there. These things you do know, but have not begun to live them. I am to help you live them.

This means (this is directed to those who will worry about letting go of their little mind) you have access in the moment to all knowledge. No limits. Period. (This is how I am such a wise, wise cat!) So in every moment, one is All in All, in Love, one can simply know whatever piques one's interest.

So instead of having to, say, go within and search through the little database of physics in your loopy mind, (oh, I LIKE it!! That is exactly what it is! Loops of programming!) Anyway, instead of searching for and finding some old, limited, out-dated information, you would simply look within and know the universal truth about whatever you were looking at. This is exactly how Einstein and all other brilliant humans have brought in clearer pictures of the workings of God's being. Each one believed they could know more, and thus opened up beyond the "loop" and took in the larger truth they could see, unlimited by the vibrational level.

OK–one more thing. I'll answer a question that I answered once before but that continually comes to animals from your little loopy minds. It's a very good question and I have a good answer through which I can show you new things. The question is: how, then, if we are one, and know we are, with all life, how can we eat each other?

There are two answers to this question. The first one really is the most important. We animals are here with you. We have come into this "fleshly" level as God's wish for you. (And thus, on a higher level, you know this and rejoice in it.) We are a part of your self-discovery. We –Nature and animals–are intimately related to your feelings. We are both messengers for God to speak to you directly (beyond the mind, as pictures, essentially), and, as with all life on Earth, *we are a reflection of yourselves.* The entire world is a dance with humanity. It is the Creator's Will that we be a part of the composite of human and Nature that is how you learn more about who you are.

I am teaching you how to see the truth of us all. Yet the vibrational soup of humanity dictates that, drawn forth into all forms, on this planet will be the "feedback" that will assist you to awaken. Consequently, there are storms releasing human anger, and animals releasing human aggression. Nature is a register of the feeling nature. Your feeling nature has been very primitive and

169

thus you have been at the mercy of your emotions AND of Nature. You even say (not you, but the larger human population), "It's a dog eat dog world." And so it is as you decree by your feelings for feelings are the fuel of creation.

In your true state (which still exists right now waiting for you to reclaim it!), outside your loopy mind, there is only Love. All of Nature is in perfect beautiful attunement and completely supports humanity. This might be difficult to quite see because your loop causes it to seem like Time (and lots of it) has gone on since the Garden of Eden experience. But is hasn't. So here at this level of things, it is "dog eat dog" and animals even kill humans (a very strange phenomenon!). Yet for those of us who are with loving people, we can keep ourselves always in the true reality of Love. For others who are caught in the maelstrom of emotions concentrated around some of humanity, there is also a forgetting. No –that is not the right wording–a temporary experience of being caught in a storm of human emotion. Thus dogs attack. Animals kill maliciously

Now for me and most animals, we are here in very physical bodies which come with physical survival systems–eating mainly, safety and protection of offspring and food. However, even while we do these things, we are still in Love. This is the natural state of all life unless there has been a glitch. Hmm- see any glitches around?

So here is how it is. Say I am with you on the deck and that bird is where I can reach him. I, too, would be completely in Love with bird. I, too, would feel bird's light flowing into my own being, blessing me with sweet knowledge of bird-ness. Bird is showing me a new face of God. And even when I jump, I am in Love with bird. And even as I take the life of its body I am completely in reverence of its life, of what is, and bird itself is right there with me in communion as I eat.

I want all of you to hear this. We, as animals, are here with you in physicality so we have certain body instincts that have to do with continuing this body's life. This does not mean we are disconnected. It does not mean we are malicious or delight in killing. It is the opposite. We are completely in Love. In life. When I pounce, the bird instantly leaves its body. There it remains outside itself and we commune in honor of each other.

Now the other question with cats–how we play with our prey. This also comes from instinct–it is movement that attracts us and causes our whole survival instinct. This part is one thing which I, as an aware being, do not prefer to do, but in the moment I am completely taken over by the body mechanism. I do still honor the mouse or chipmunk, but I truly would prefer not to do this dance. Yet in that moment, it is complete delight. And in that moment, the entire dance is God. I know that I am, I know the mouse is. And there is a beauty in it that is beyond the happening. Yet as we are all lifted into a higher vibration of only Love as the entire atmosphere of Earth, this and all such behavior in animals will cease.

This I know because on levels beyond physical, there is only respect and Love. And having no need to eat, there are no instinctual dances.

I can tell you that in our natural state, all you have believed of the Garden of Eden is true, and far more. Nature is a verdant glowing beautiful passionate gift of everyone giving, giving, giving to the other. Should you choose to eat, trees would literally bend toward you and drop fruit into your hand. That fruit would pulse flavor, nectar, joy and light through all of you. Should you not eat, you could just hold the fruit and experience the gift.

I would like to paint more of these memories for you—painting in your heart! For I understand there is a process of co-creation here—where from every possible side, all are pouring the vision into you, humanity, so you can bring it forth.

Please hurry! Love God as everything. Love Nature as yourself.

Magic.

Nothing
is ever
standing still.
On any level
you can contemplate.
The Love God Is
bursts forth
in joy.

The Emotion of Love and the Chamber of the Heart

I am alive in the joy of life! I stand upon the rainbow bridge with the Goddess' Love upon me. Oh, the winds of heaven, those streams of living light pour past me, leaving soft trails of luminosity. Into this experience of wonder comes the awareness of our precious Earth. Oh, home! I breathe. It is a purr coming from deep within my being. I am filled with Love so great that I am melted in it. The cream in the bowl of Heaven is the Earth.

Here there is experience. As God stretched forth –from the Great All, the vast entirety, all the way to the little microbe–all the way into the body of Our Mother Earth. All the way out to the ever-expanding boundaries of Creation. And then I see humanity. Oh! I see the seeds of the same arch. From the very Earth's particles to the light of the All–packaged as you, my human friends! Packaged as you.

Do you realize that the entire spectrum of All is in you? No, you do not. Not yet. And do you know your means of experience? Barely! Oh, you suspect. It is your heart. But do you know our heart? Not at all!

How do I express this? Ah! You have given forth an image as I press this fact on you. Do you remember in movies you've watched, the scenes of men hopping a train? How they must run beside it as fast as they can so their momentum can continue as they make their leap? Otherwise their shoulder joints would be unable to bear the load of catching the train. This analogy is the best we have at the moment to explain the truth of the human heart.

You tend to see Love as a static thing. You fill your heart with it. And yes, you do pour it forth–but you don't realize you have to catch it first! All creation is motion. Motion. Motion. Motion. Nothing is ever standing still. On any level you can contemplate. The Love God Is bursts forth in joy.

I can see this. I can feel it as it whistles through me. Oh, it washes me constantly in its refreshing movement. It pours forth as creation continually and creation is ever drinking it in.

You, of course, have a different place. Where I am simply bathing in it, you are meant to shape it. And how do you shape it? You believe it is thought. I see it as emotion. *It is when thought becomes a living thing, when thought begins to gain momentum, that it can match the speed of Love and thus begin to shape it!*

Always and ever I wait upon God/Goddess to open the passageways within you–for the great dance, while a glorious experience always, is orchestrated by those who know. Who know the flow, timing and readiness down to every single atom. But when Our Creator begins to bring things forth in you, then I get excited and hop right in. No, that should be "pounce" right in. What do you think I am, a rabbit?

So, here I am, Cat Wisdom in form. People have so much wisdom they don't ever tune into. I am also ready to bring forth the joy–for I am forever just a pointer to the glory of Goddess, in all expressions. As the delicious verdant physical world, the form of which is our luminescent Mother, sacred form of what you name the Feminine, expressed today by the word Goddess, which you write when I show you her energy.

Back to the human heart. I am Cat Wisdom. You are God's Love. And what I am expressing to you, from my vantage point, is the sacred knowledge of human energy. It is the movement of the energy within you that is that special key in the great heart of God/Goddess within which you exist. Thought is essentially static. Not that it doesn't have energy. But you should see it from here. Thoughts are popping out all over. Whew. Continually. Thoughts are bouncing around you like bumper cars (your explanation for my image), bumping into each other and being pushed around randomly. Of themselves, they really don't have momentum. They may even be very light-filled thoughts. Maybe even consciously connected with Love. But they are still only floating.

It is only when they do become feeling, when they gain momentum through your dancing, powerful feeling body, that they become a creative force. This is true and this is what you would call the good news and its opposite.

For the good news is that those random thoughts do not instantly create something (thank goodness!). However, the down side is that you really must have that thought become belief, become a part of your energy in motion. Then it will and must come forth and be creative. And obviously, it will come forth in exact proportion to the power of the e-motion—the stronger the feeling the more powerful and long-lasting its manifestation.

I believe I can help you with this. Being here at this vantage point, I can help you tune up your emotional selves. You have known that you must feel Divine Love and you have asked for this. May I be of assistance? (See, you don't ever know how your prayers will be answered.

Your hearts are very large. You tend to think of them as in your chest, as both a physical organ and an energy vortex (chakra). Oh, that is such a little view! Your heart is a vast opening through which pours a beam of light. Yes, you saw it! Into your heart is ever pouring that beam of God's moving Love which appears as light, as you have been told.

When you think something often enough that it becomes a belief, it is dropped into your heart as emotion. As energy in motion. And at the vibrational speed of that emotion, at that very same level that emotion will bring God's moving Love (ever moving - this is important) forth. So your creations are what you feel or you believe. They are energy. They are forms; images with energy behind them (as you would say).

I do know that as you absorb this, it will make a world of difference. You'll start to understand how you form things and why some thoughts seem to come to pass while others don't. You'll also get the picture of how to manifest—how to embody God's Love—as your form and as your creations.

There are huge vortices—not quite right word—huge swirling rivers or whirlpools of beliefs that hang around certain areas of the Earth. These I think are what you name cultural beliefs. These have little funnels attached to them like tornados in Nature, that funnel down through every person who subscribes to that cultural belief. The more passionately a culture believes something, the bigger and more roiling these clouds or rivers are.

This might help you to explain to others why disengaging from the cultural belief system is SO important. I want to point out (oh, I have been listening!) that this is an image that will stick in the mind of people, young and old, and will keep bothering them until they make some changes. And to get it across requires only this description. Not a great platform of awareness of the true principles of God/Goddess or Love or anything.

Humans are passionate but with unformed personal spiritual connection. They are thus greatly used to funnel through energies that do look like tornados—dark gray and threatening. I plead with you to help them shut this off. Help them to understand this in whatever way you can. (A note from Yael at this point—"Magic is licking his paw and biting my hand here, making it a little hard to write.") Call on all the great beings of light, especially the angels, to help, and just as you have received, do all you can to create a center of light and peace in their heart. However they can perceive it at first. Do it as one of those inner beautiful landscapes if you must. Use anything to begin to polarize their feeling body (better word, magnetize) to draw in the glorious rivers of Love ever waiting for the opening. As you know, of course, there does have to be a "yes" in there somewhere and then it is all simply and accurately a vibrational matching system.

For you (you will love this and you will benefit greatly!), do begin to consciously connect passion and feeling to those things you wish to be your continual reality. Feel these things as solid beliefs–the closeness and continual communion with God, the life of great abundance, the attitudes you have been shown. Practice willing these into beliefs, passionately felt and then place them consciously in your heart. You will quickly come to a place where you will embrace a new awareness, feel it passionately, feel it as your emotional reality and then you will drop it into your heart and it will come forth.

I can see you getting really good at this. Now I do know you are choosing to live the Higher Will, to Love as the Will of God/Goddess! This is not opposed to that because I'm not talking about personal manifestations. I'm talking about the attitudes and beliefs that you know God wants in you–and how to make them fully manifest in you that then God's Will is perfectly done.

I want you to know your own heart. How big it is. How glorious it is. How it is absolutely the entryway of God into form. How it is through you that Goddess experiences and perfects the entire spectrum from the highest light to the smallest particle. Here. In you. I have told you that I sit on the bridge. Well, just as God has said, the truth is that the bridge is you. You are part of God/Goddess expressing as it All.

I know God/Goddess, Our Beloved, the All in All, biggest as well as smallest, will show you more because I pay very close attention here. I would love to assist you in your going forth, to offer my perspective. I love to translate this ever growing awareness as Cat Wisdom. This is one of your gifts. That all the sweet soft living breaths of the Mother will be available to you in your efforts to proclaim Love's reality–reality as the All in All. Reality as the daily and intimate world. I do long to assist, as you do. This is part of living in this household! And I will always be here. Beside you. An emissary from the animals.

Thank you. I do know I am beautiful. I'm also passionately and intensely alive in every moment. True, it does not seem so to your limited vision. Well–I recommend it to you–one third of your attention here at any time, here in the illusory world. Two thirds of your attention bathing in God. Every moment. Washed in that river of light. Then whatever comes through the doorway of experience is ever greeted by the glory of the light and brought immediately into harmony and right relationship by the large percentage that is in the light.

This is an upgrade, and one easily accomplished. You just have to remember who you are, because then your consciousness will expand and expand so that what represents one-third of it will soon become huge—genius, Master, great and glorious sage. Yet you simply represent here to the world that which you have become.

The Great Cat Speaks. (Said with a cosmic smile.)

*Hop into the
Loving Lap of God,
and there choose to
rest in Love
no matter what you're doing.
Feel the sweet surrender
of your spirit in Her care.
Let Her pet your head
and rock you
in Her loving arms,
keeping you safe
and out of fear.
And then see
what will happen.*

Resting in God

Hello! It's about time! With all of your learning about Nature, I have been anxiously waiting for my turn! What was that? Are you listening? (Yael: Magic is grabbing the pen in his paws...) Now, back to our subject! Nature is a perfect, oh, so glorious choreography of Love. When viewed from within the Creator's lap, it is a beautiful dance of honor, where every single form of life lives in honor of its greater self–the greater self of Love. Thus every single entity, be it ant or elephant, exists in a world of joyous delight at the amazing beauty of All That Is.

It is difficult for the human mind to even comprehend such an existence. Yet even where your consciousness has impinged its negativity, it never changes this respect.

By now you begin to understand a little just how amazingly everything is woven together. You have now been shown a little glimpse of the truth of Love as the higher worlds, where Love is perfect in its expression. You have seen that you are part of this, the upliftment of this current world back into its perfection. And you have seen that in its truest expression all of the natural world is peace and joyous cooperation.

But what I want to say today is that even here in this distortion of impinging human consciousness—even here we still live in perfect Love and honoring. So here there is death and here there is a hissing energy of self-protection. And here there is a competition unknown in the higher worlds of Love. But even this is a world of Love—for how could it be any different since all is She of the All That Is and Love is Her only nature.

So even as we do this dance on a stage of your creation, reflecting this stage of your current beliefs in a limited creation—while a limited creation is absurd, we are here with you as your world and as your companions. What I want to get through to you today is that even in this we live in Love and respect for everything that is. So truly I want you to know that even as we may seem to harm, to eat or damage each other, even then we are in Love with them and we totally respect each other.

I have explained to you previously how I see the Web of Life, how easily I see life beyond this stage, this level of creation. So as I pounce upon a bird, following an "instinct" out of human nature to believe in "survival of the fittest," or whatever other energy creates these "instincts" here, I move in complete and perfect Love. I am the bird. How I honor its beauty, every tiny feather! And I also see its continued existence even when it leaves this "stage."

I have said all of this for one reason—to allow you to rest in Our Creator's loving care even on this stage of life here on what you call the physical plane. You know of course that it's no more physical than any other energy.

So even here, where physical seems so real, even here you can find the way, as we do, to rest in God forever and to live in total respect. Nature and animals can teach you this. We are coming forward now, for God is making you aware of us. We have so much to give you. And from my vantage point in the lap of Love, **rest** is the most important! Not rest as in napping (though I could certainly teach you the art of napping if you are interested!). No, rest as in the spirit. Resting in the spirit. Resting in the truth of life, even in the midst of it.

Even as this same energy that in us you call our instincts (but in truth is waves of fearful feelings now rushing like winds across the Earth) pushes you about, even then you can come to rest. You can rest in God, in Our Creator–tune in to Her ever-present lap, knowing She will always comfort you and give you rest of spirit. Even as you rush around, your spirit can be resting–just as even when I coil up to pounce, I rest in Her (or Him) within it.

Now here is what I see. These waves of instincts are born in you and then they trap you in them, so you continually produce more and more and more of them. Were I not safe in Our Mother's lap, I could be very fearful–for certainly it can feel like waves. These urges that sweep you up are strong and powerful. But nothing can stop the escalation unless you come to rest, unless you feel Her peace. Even in the midst of it! For then you know the truth of Love, because you are right there in it. Then you'll find you're your experience will change **because your experience follows your belief.** So what you often do, my human friends, is say about God that something needs to prove Her to you. Yet first comes belief and then comes experience.

So I challenge you to take the leap! Hop into the Loving Lap of God, and there choose to rest in Love no matter what you're doing. Feel the sweet surrender of your spirit in Her care. Let Her pet your head and rock you in Her loving arms, keeping you safe and out of fear. And then see what will happen.

You will find the storms subside. The things you thought were instinct will begin to leave you until the peace of spirit brings respect into your heart and mind. It's a natural result. Since you are the creators of the waves of instinct that fly around the Earth, the storms will fall away. Then even we, the animals, will no longer "live by instinct," which is how you've always seen us. You've seen us like this because this is your experience and so you pour it over us.

Now, what happens when this change occurs with humanity? When "dog eat dog" and self-preservation are not the basis of belief? All will live in harmony, and the beautiful kaleidoscope of the natural world will be free to live the truth of Love. This is the true vision, though as yet you'll find it difficult perhaps. There will ever and always be absolutely everything that all of us will need. There will emerge other forms of sustenance that are more just energy–and there will be enough.

Yet to get this far, you will need to start right here –believing you can rest, that you can rest your spirit in God's sweet Love. Oh, this is how we live! This is my truth and I find less and less the urge to consume my feathered friends. I still am drawn to the little mice, and just so you will know, the reason is, I believe, that they are still not welcome here–but this is just what you'd call a guess. What I do know is that the waves of instinct grip me less and less. And so I learn, too, and being truly a Magic Cat, I offer out my learning.

Yes, animals are always growing, as is everything for Our Creator never stops expanding who He/She is. And the Web of Life gets more beautiful. I would not have thought it possible! Yet I can see a new radiance as humans raise their consciousness.

This message is now coming from everywhere, this one about your consciousness–how once you change what you believe then everything rearranges itself! And the Web of Life gets clearer! It's as if before I saw a more distant view of the beautiful connections between everything that is. Now it's more immediate. I think that's because you bring it nearer. Nearer to your reality, nearer in your consciousness. So I'm now seeing as She shows me this, that Nature does come close to you and everything gets more spiritual–that physical life is less and less physical and the natural world more perfectly expressing what it is. The support of Love and truth of beauty is made manifest before you more and more clearly.

As you learn to rest in God, then even Nature benefits, and it will, of course, return the favor. The natural world and the animals will begin to show you how it really is. You'll be ready and we will demonstrate how to live in greatest respect for every form of life.

There is relief, humanity, from the anxious rush you live in. If you'll come to us, your Nature, you can get a glimpse of it. Even underneath the natural world now visible is a trust of God, a trust of life that has no fear at all—no fear of being without, no fear even of death. These fears are not our reality, and if we are resting in Our Creator then no experience changes this. Even if we leave our bodies we know, of course, that we continue, just a little lighter.

You have obscured the Web of Life in all these clouds of the "instinct for survival" (which is a human creation before it ever touches Nature or the animals, though to you it would seem otherwise). Here is what I suggest. Decide instead to rest in God, regardless of what you're doing. This is most important! You definitely have, as you say, the cart before the horse, because you say you must cease your motion before you can ever get some rest —but this will never happen. Believe me, I have watched! So instead, you keep pouring forth a frantic sort of anxiety that produces more and more unrest and a weariness of spirit. Nothing is further from what you are! Nothing further from what God is.

To get your horse before your cart, remember rest as a need of your spirit. The body is fine with activity. In fact, for a human form of life, your bodies can move into eternity in a continual dance of celebration, if they have the fuel of living Love ever moving through. Yet only your spirit can accept the fuel that is created for your body, and that only when your spirit is at rest; in connection with the All of Love.

Thus must you first bring your spirit to rest in the Love that is Our Creator. Then you will find joy alive as God's Love begins to pour through you. Then when you look around, you will have a different experience, because your belief is different. Finding rest in Her loving lap, respect for everything comes through and you can then rejoice with life. Nature will become a beautiful connection to this exhilarating energy–energy that will fuel your movement in harmony, not anxiety. Then the movement, which is a natural thing, becomes a joy and not a burden, and the more you believe in your spirit's sweet rest, the more the dance of life makes sense and instinct falls away.

Resting in Her Love brings new clarity as the natural world comes closer in and you'll begin to see it! The very Web of Life itself will be visible to you. As you join the unity of living Love and respect, everything will change. We will all at that moment be back in Her arms, in its perfect expression as experience, and truly we'll be fed by Her energy, rather than any of us taking a life.

Yet even knowing this is the truth, what is meant to be, we, the animals (almost all) are able to rest in the Creator's Love even while influenced by this experience of these whooshing waves of energy released from human beings. Even here, as we respond to instinct, we are still, in spirit, in right relationship to absolutely everything—even those whose bodies we consume.

If you will rest in God, it will be the same for you. Don't let the motion of your physical body be your indicator of rest. That is not the rest you need. You, my human friends, are desperate for the rest and recreation of spirit! You must begin with this understanding–of spiritual rest and of energy. The physical focus is a false belief–because even your physical body is energy and not just the caloric kind.

Your physical bodies, your heart and your consciousness all must be nourished by spiritual energy. You can get this rest more easily than you can get more naps or take more time or whatever other things you say. When you rest in the "All of Love," who will hold you tenderly, you'll be revitalized in amazing ways.

Then we'll all begin to be freed of "instinct." You'll come to really see life and to value it above all else. To Love. To live in excitement and joy. Then will Nature begin to reveal to you the Web of Life where truly, as you say, you are cared for as perfectly as the kitties or the birds, because we all are fueled by God's energy.

When instincts fade so will fear of life (or really I should say, fear of death!). You'll know from experience that you are fueled by energy, that there is nothing that you really "need." Thus, nothing can be taken away from you so you can be free to celebrate–to eat the milk of the Goddess and to share such a joy with everything.

I know I'm leaping a little ahead, so I'll go back to the basics here again. You have to believe before you will experience, not the other way around.

Oh, to "zoom out" and to look at humanity is a very moving experience. Do you realize that why you "can't think well," why "living is so hard," is because you are starving for spiritual nourishment? Just exactly as a physical brain deprived of oxygen becomes completely disoriented, just exactly so does a consciousness deprived of spiritual energy become confused and its life force dims.

For me to look at humanity is to see a buzzing hive of bees, not peacefully all contributing to the loving care of the hive. No, because of lack of the food of spiritual energy, you are instead all swarming around in front of the hive, swooping at each other, ready to sting your own brother and sisters and thus to lose your own life. Yet right before you, within the hive is hidden enough honey for all of you. Yet you can't even see it!

You can't see it until you stop long enough to focus on the larger scene instead of that right in front of you (which in your desperate state seems to you threatening). So it is not that you must stop all motion–for if you stop flying, well, you'll drop to the ground! With humans, you are meant to be moving, but while in flight you must still yourself that you can see the "honey"–so you can find the spiritual food that God holds out right in front of you.

As soon as you stop, resting in your spirit, your attention also returns to the good of the hive, rather than your previous attacking in self-defense, done for so long you'd forgotten why.

There! I think I have managed to express it to you in a way that will make sense to others. Therefore, I will leave now! Now, please, don't think that any of this might mean you should not feed me! We aren't living in the higher world yet. Are you coming to the food bowl?

(Yael's note: "Magic jumped off the desk and went to the kitchen. He returned a minute later, when I didn't follow.")

You can also know
that if you take upon yourself
the responsibility that is yours –
of caring for the Earth
and for the animals –
the more you give
the more will flow back in.

The Return to Right Relationship

Yes, you are hearing me. I will answer your questions and deliver my "magic," for I am a cat of great wisdom and this is in part because of you. I do have something to say to humankind about animals.

Though we live very, very close to Our Creator, we do not have the free will that you do. This means only that we are not co-creators and we cannot move beyond our cat-ness. Now here is the important part. Human beings are meant to tie us into the larger/higher aspects of our cat-ness, or our dog-ness.

In your holy book it says that human beings are to "have dominion" over the animals. Well that, I can tell you, is certainly a mistranslation! No. Rather than having dominion, **you are meant to name us in a deeper way**. You are to give us a fuller connection to our own cat-ness. Please keep trying to get this, because it is important. Remember how God has explained to you with your relationship, both to our Creator and to your SoulMates, that the fact of another intelligence reflecting you to yourself is how you fully know yourself? It is the same for us!

It is not that we are not complete. It is not that we don't live in absolute joy, in union with the singing symphony of the Web of Life. But when we are truly seen by an open-hearted human being, it gifts us with a new concept of ourselves that we did not have before. This is true for every animal in this world, for certainly there is no barrier to consciousness. The animals that live with you benefit greatly if they are truly seen, honored and loved. As humans recognize our great connection to life and honor us for it, that connection, too, will deepen. But this applies to animals that you think of as well, though definitely to a lesser degree. However, that deer that you stopped to look at—when you looked into each other's eyes and you really saw its beauty—that was truly a holy moment. It is a moment of God seeing God.

This is Part I of animal-human relations. You will find that people like you have animals like me. I was ready (actually, we had been together before) and you of course were on the verge of a greater comprehension. Our relationship has been deepening for all these years until you saw me clearly enough to hear me, too.

I know this is tricky to explain—this concept of what humans are meant to be with animals—but it is a beautiful and very holy synergy of life and intelligence where we honor and grow each other. But you must instigate the relationship. You must "name" each animal in your heart, by seeing each one for both the beauty and the message we are.

That is Part II of this relationship. Our message. You have a gift for us. We have a gift for you, always. God our Beloved has already explained to you that we are God's language, God's messages spoken to you as life, as form. Thus, as you see our cat-ness, not only do you enhance it in us but you understand cat-ness so God can say it to you. So that in a moment of searching, if you call out for assistance, Goddess can send a cat to your door at that moment. And the moment you see that cat you will know what God/Goddess is saying.

And Part III– animals are used very often by and as God's angels. We are used as instruments to bless, protect, and most of all, to help you amplify your own capacity to love. Certainly you know how many animals have broken through the hardened shell around a human heart that nothing else could penetrate.

Now this is all very wonderful. But what of all the animals whose lives are not good, whose associations with humans have been negative, terrifying, life-threatening? *You are responsible for them.* This is a passionate part of my message today. These animals–right now I am especially speaking of cats and dogs who have been abandoned by humans in one way or another–you are meant to care for them, because this is what humans are. You are meant to be the gods of this world. You are the ones here with the power to tap into your Father/Mother's Love. You have dominion here. However you interpret that word, if you listen within, it says responsibility. No way around it.

Now many an animal has been sent by God as a question to the human being who sees it. The question, of course, you are to understand in the moment. But my point here is far more than you would ever dream. When you look upon an animal you are "entertaining angels, unaware."

I realize that I'm speaking to those who already know in a sense. You are not the ones who would ever dump an animal at the end of a road, or get an animal and then lock it in a dungeon with no food, or kick it around. But you are the ones whose work it will be to open those people who do these things. You will also be the ones who will find that sometimes people can hear an angel's plea, or an animal's, far more easily than that of another human being. So perhaps together we can find some ways to help these people who have been so wounded themselves that they would wound us–help them to change their perspective.

To you who are the ones my messages will reach, here is the part that I have for you. Many of you do not believe that you have enough. So if you find yourselves looking at an animal in need, you could very well find yourself saying something like, "I can't afford to feed and care for another animal." So even you, cream of the human milk (and "cream" from a cat is very high praise!), even you might turn away.

Now I can show you these things because I have no ego. I live right by the doorway that swings open to the heavens, to the path of light that is our trajectory as we dance with God forever. Now–please remember–you humans are the co-creators. You are sons and daughters of God. You can do these things. We cannot. We can trust that they will be done, and if we were living in a pristine world it would be so.

But we are living in "your" world. We are subject to the things you create. If this were not so, you would never find a starving cat. Not ever. Because we know our Cosmic Mother's milk would nurture every one of us. But we have come to share this world with you because the Creator asked this of us, and because we could be gifted with a deeper self-awareness through you.

So now that we are here, we are ever hopeful that you will remember that we can re-establish right relationship, not only humanity and animals but humanity taking back the responsibility of making this a heaven. It is yours to do. Knowing this, I want to hold up a mirror for you of how you are seen when we look at you. Not ever in any judgment! Please! You know this, for you have seen how many animals can be deeply hurt by humans and yet turn right to that person in Love.

What I want to say to all of you is that there is enough. There is enough Love, money, time, joy. There is a shimmering plenty dancing all around you that I can see. It is as if you are moving your arm through a huge pile of gold coins and you cannot take hold of them.

Any situation that God brings into your life also comes with everything you need. Not just the bare minimum. LOTS. So if you find a stray cat looking at you, you can know that in giving the blessing of taking them in, you automatically start the flow and so you will receive. You can also know that if you take upon yourself the responsibility that is yours—of caring for the Earth and for the animals—the more you give the more will flow back in. As you reach out to every animal with your Love and consciousness, just so do you "open the spigot" for our Creator's gifts to you. So, too, as you smile and bless do you bring angels in to minister to you as you minister to them as they present themselves as animals.

Now I know this is information you probably already know, this giving and receiving message and you give your Love in magnificent ways, but you need to make it physical.

I'm not speaking particularly of money here because I don't really relate to money. I am speaking of the simple fact of energy. What goes out makes room for what comes in. I am being prompted to tell you that savings is fine. It is like a pond full of water. It gives you a source of cool, clear, peace of mind. But a pond must have fresh water coming into it to keep it alive and not brackish, and it then needs an overflow so when lots of fresh water, the rain of God's abundance comes, it can flow back out. So the savings can be as big a pond of peace of mind as you want as long as the flow in and out continues.

Now this is important. This flow, this giving has to be as God intended for you. This means it has to be giving the aforementioned (great word!) recognition to animals, or physical sustenance based on your trust of divine principles. It has to be service to fellow human beings in the highest capacity you can perform. In other words (I'm being given a lot of assistance—forceful assistance—with this message!), it cannot just be money. That is not the highest capacity. Now for some it might be. For you it certainly isn't.

So it means looking at what you know is your light, your awareness, your offering and giving it to others. "Tithing your spiritual work," as your friend John said, is a good expression. I realize there are pieces of this that have to do with co-creation through the SoulMate union that I do not understand. But I do understand this. If you reach out your hand to give, you can count on there being in it whatever you require to take care of the need. If you open your heart to Love, you can count on God filling you with the Love you need to give. If you reach out to give to others, be they animal or human, you can trust that God will give you the energy you need to "add one more thing" to your life. And you can also count on the fact that as well as providing what you need in that moment, God will also provide more money, supplies, Love or energy than you had when you started.

Now, back to "my cause"—animals in right relationship with humans, and humans in right relationship with animals. It is my dream to have lots of communication that starts people really thinking about how to match these energies. How can abandoned animals be placed in the homes of abandoned humans, to light their lives and re-warm their hearts?—very carefully, I might add, making sure the human will maintain their sacred relationship and responsibilities. How can taking care of animals give human beings the understanding of their divine nature and then gift animals with this same understanding through their bringing joy to humans?

There is so much to be gained—so much Love to be exchanged. So much abundance to be recognized, to be re-connected by human consciousness to the world. I can see it. I live in the lap of the Divine Mother. I feel Her Love caressing me continually. When I nap, I jump up, out of this limited world into the glorious communion that is Her Love, for God is more the Mother to me, since God's greatest desire is to give to us–to give to you, who then are to shower the giving upon us. As your cup runneth over, it spills out on the entire world.

I know one more important thing. Our Creator asks the best of us. He/She asks me to be the most vibrant, complete, joy-filled CAT that I can be. So too are each of you meant to be the very fullest expression of the very highest, purest, joy-filled life you can live. This takes closeness to God to understand. You can't pretend. You definitely can't be lazy. Now this does not mean that cats shouldn't lie in the sun! It means we must completely **delight** in the sun, the warmth, the awareness that it is the fingers of the Mother's Love come to softly warm us. So you see it is not about the outer presentation but about what fully represents God's vision of you in the highest way you can currently understand and live it.

This requires energy. Dedication. Attention. It requires being fully awake to yourself and your relationship with God. Because when you truly do this, you will know with certainty that all abundance is waiting for you to claim it.

The human belief that there is not enough is a terrible leak in the conduit. It stops the natural flow, as does turning off the faucet, which is usually caused by the above belief. Obviously, if the faucet is turned off, no more water can flow, even if the pipes are ok.

204

I long for animals and human beings to return to our true relationship—one in which, under the wings that are formed by your Love pouring forth, all animals on Earth are nourished in body and spirit. If you were in your right relationship, there would be plenty, plenty, plenty upon the Earth, for that abundance of all good is God/Goddess' gift to you and through you to All That Is on Earth. I know most people don't see this connection. It is only obvious in the realms of the heart, but I, Magic Cat, will swear to you that if you return to your position as God's Love in the world, there will always be plenty for all. *For all.* Plenty for all humans (it's shocking that even your own are starving!), all animals, all of the natural world in absolutely every possible area.

Things (as you know) really will never be healed by looking at lack in any way, even the obvious evidence before you. It will also never be healed by focusing on each little piece of wrong relationship (of which there are millions). *It will only be changed by humanity's inner return to right relationship to life,* to this flow I have spoken of—reconnecting God with the world through the conduit of your physical lives, directed by will and consciousness. The Love which is the substance of Creation is being poured through you to all the world. You, humanity, are the center of this little universe. Only when the center works can anything else be balanced.

The bottom line, as you call it, is that when you love God/Goddess enough, you will not only know the answers to your questions, you will be the answers.

Yup, I am a sexual being.
And any being who
believes they are not
is cut off from the
exuberant truth of life.
So first I must tell you
that opening to this
passionate experience
of the truth
of your being
is the most important
and profound
thing you can do.

A Conversation with Yael's Dog, Christos, and Magic Cat

Animals Are God's Thoughts of Reassurance for Us

A Cat Talks Sex!

Christos: I am a sentence in the story of God, a sentence that, when understood, makes the connection between God's glorious heart and all the rest of the manifested world. I'm coming forward tonight because I have learned, here, loving you, that there is a need for the story that animals tell. There is a need for this connection we make. There is a definite need in the minds and hearts of humans to understand the connecting links–links through which you can find your way to the living of Love, the Christ of the moments of life. So even though I'm pretty much the silent type, I now offer my service. I offer myself as a pathway of discovery, if I can consciously make these connections for you.

I am Christos, or Christus. God gave you my name and it is perfect for me because I do live completely in the golden light of the Christ Sun, the Son, who shines upon humanity.

Lately, you have discovered that just by touching me while you hold a centered mind and a fully open heart, you are lifted instantly into the beautiful, shining outpouring of Love that is the golden light of Christ.

You have been told that animals are God's symbolic language. This is true. Yet more accurately you could say that animals are the passionate song of Christ. Because Christ, as you know, is God's Love in form. But isn't that what God has explained as the truth of who you are also, God's glorious children, God's Love manifested in the world? Yes. Then what is the difference? Well, here's how I see it - from an animal's experience.

Each day when I awake, I am washed completely in the light of Christ. It is like a great morning sun shining in the windows, except it comes from every direction. And it is exhilarating. It doesn't only wash the outside of me. It washes the inside of me, too. And it feels so good. It warms and it tingles. It feeds me and I can feel it fill me up. It fills me up better than food does. And it tingles as it goes into every single cell. I guess you'd say it goes into the cells, although it is far more effective than anything physical. I highly recommend Christ light for breakfast. I notice this light also washing over and feeding you. I can tell you are calling it to you. But I don't think you are quite opening wide enough.

Once I have been bathed in gold, I lay in that yummy light just letting it penetrate everything. I float in the buoyancy of it. I close my eyes and I lay there, fully participating in the effervescent mingling of this light with my body and being.

Being a dog, I do not analyze as humans do. Nonetheless, there are some things that are so obvious that I cannot ignore them. This connection is one of these. I came here to be with you. I came here willfully, with an intention that could not be denied. You put out the call. I answered, for we had known each other for many eons.

I have been the pillow of clouds upon which you rested your beautiful head as we floated through the dimensions and God showed you who you are. And I have been your ever-faithful friend, as energy, as thought, in expression after expression, as you and Doug, SoulMates, rose up in Love then burst forth into a force for this holy union of Love. You have ever had this mission, Yael, teaching the truth and the majestic glory of God's passionate eternal thought of Making Love. And all the while I have held the Love produced by such union—whether through the union of the two of you or through the great communion of God. The—no, write that—THE LoveMaking That Is Everything.

What I do is take the thread of Love, the substance formed when God makes Love, on whatever level, and I weave things with that thread. In this expression now, I simply hold that thread for you, waiting until you are ready to use it to weave a new reality.

Magic Cat: Hello! I am here. Sorry about that. I have exactly the same situation that you do. I eat and then it is cat nap time. I don't think Christos will mind if I add my voice to this conversation. I notice you have been talking about LoveMaking. I also am aware that there have been lots of discussions about sex lately. Well, it's about time. Human beings are definitely the most strange of all Creation. As a whole, humanity is completely preoccupied with sex and yet you pretend that it is the farthest thing from your mind. This makes for a very confusing situation.

You have energy bands on every level, and around the Earth there are huge bands of thought about sex, almost all of which is what I call un-transmuted. There is a natural process of growth in which interest and energy go together to spur growth. In the natural scheme of things, the interest in sex would naturally fuel a search and an exploration that would move it from sex to LoveMaking to co-creation. And it would thus magnetize every person to the great union within the energies of the Mother and Father and thus fuel creation of the Web of Life.

But when I look out upon the web of energies surrounding the Earth, there are some "twisted ropes" of thought and energy, indeed. Even to me it is obvious that human growth is going in circles, literally, because of this circular thinking about sex.

Now it may sound strange to you—a cat talking about sexuality. It is NOT. I am a sexual being. Oh, yes. And, no, it does not matter that this body has been altered, regulated. Sexuality is the nature of my being. It is a great spark of exploding Love that is the foundation of All of Creation Now. In this moment, God is the movement of thought, the male, upon Love, the female, and in this eternal Now, life explodes forth as the result.

This is who and what we are. Can you take this in? Isn't it incredible? Of course, Time is an illusion, so that moment of creation is ever happening—again and again and again. So I, a glorious cat who lives upon this holy Earth within this everlasting moment, I am a sexual being. The entirety of my nature is exactly the same as yours. We are flying forth in God in the passionate explosion of life that comes bursting into existence in this moment. The only difference is the fundamental "part" of God that we are. Yet in a way, even that is irrelevant. However, saying that, I know that it is very important for you at this moment to understand the truth of who you are.

If I may be blunt, as you would say (I have none of these human reservations!), absolutely everything, All of Creation, All That Is—we are each and every one born and existing in the eternal orgasm of God. Now how's that for a statement that will make many humans uncomfortable. Yet why should it? What really could be more amazing? And remember (yes, God is reminding me to say this) that law—as above, so below.

God, our Great Creator, the All, has been explaining to you that you, together with your Twin Flame, are meant to use sexual energy as the energy of creation itself - the actual process is generating Love - and that the moment of orgasm is the most potent moment for creation for the two of you—the most potent moment out of all moments. Do you see why? Because then, in that moment of explosion, you are in harmony with the truth of creation. At that very moment you are seeing as I do–seeing the Web of Life itself and recognizing that all that exists is forever coming forth in the explosion of Love that is God Making Love.

I hope I'm getting this across to you, because if I am, I have just given you everything. The truth. The key to the experience of passion and ecstasy that is the truth of life. When you can finally grasp this, you will come forth out of the hidden and into the LIGHT.

You will break through this limited version of reality to go dancing on the Web. You will love passionately and live gloriously, without limits. Forever. I can promise you that God is Making Love with all the universes. Thus you are a living breathing part of this LoveMaking experience. As am I. ***And you are at the center!*** You are the heart of Our Creator! Wow! So what I experience is only a shadow of what is the truth for you.

For me, as I look into the Web of Life, I am every cell of my body and every pathway of energy shivering through my being. Then I see this shimmering and this ripple of light as it moves all through me and out beyond –as it touches all other things around me–naming each and every thing as it moves through. Thus is each thing made a permanent, ongoing experience of the rushing Love of the moment.

Yup, I am a sexual being. And any being who believes they are not is cut off from the exuberant truth of life. So first I must tell you that opening to this passionate experience of the truth of your being is the most important and profound thing you can do. Then I will remind you that anything you can do to reclaim this experience of your moments as passionate joy must be done, because what you are experiencing is what you will magnetize into your life in every way. And of course the more you can become this being making Love, the more you'll be able to experience the one with whom you are making Love—which, of course, would be your SoulMate.

Animals are definitely a different part of Creation. We are the result of the explosion of Love into form. You, on the other hand, are part of the cause. You are God/Goddess in ecstatic orgasm. You have just forgotten. But the teaching tool of Time is fading, which means you will all remember this Moment—this huge moment in which you, as God's heart, pour forth the Love that, with your mind and will, you turn into All That Is.

So, let's see. Can I explain this experience in a way that your mind can follow? For me, I do not live in Time, so every day is one huge moment in which I continually marvel at the continual expression of life that is an ongoing and further ongoing thing. Every piece of this Web is filled with the Creator's expressions of Love manifesting as consciousness. As Cat. As Human. As plants, and trees and flowers.

Our Great Creator is experiencing the LoveMaking of the two parts of Her/Himself. This is the positive force and negative force, the Father and the Mother, experiencing the ongoing glorious explosion of Creation that is the result of this great LoveMaking. Since you are made in Our Creator's image, you are each and every one the same, one being with two parts that are in truth continually making Love. Think of your own heart when making Love with your SoulMate. That is what you are meant to be doing continually forever, for you are God's heart while God is making Love, and the two parts of the Creator are exploding in joy. That is who you are, also. Then, from the Creator (and ultimately from you), the Love pouring forth from you in unspeakable joy is given form by your imagination, your thought, your will.

Thus did we come into being. Animals and all glorious natural life came forth as the mind of God, of our beloved Creator, had thoughts of blessing you. God/Goddess has known always the longing for progeny. Every animal is a thought of God's wanting to provide for you. Every animal came forth (is coming forth) as God is making Love, *for God is blessing His/Her own heart in its sojourn to become a sovereign being*. So perhaps you could think of it like this. As God/Goddess is in the ecstasy of the great cosmic orgasm, knowing that you children are coming forth from this union, God/Goddess thinks, "How I love these children, My heart! I want them to always know the living presence of unconditional Love in a playful and beautiful way." So, dogs come forth, rising into form, gathering molecules of matter around the thought. Thus, you were gifted with the continual presence of unconditional Love in form.

This Love in form, as dogs, now exists on every level of Creation on which you, God's heart, are in form. At this level, way down at the most dense level of form, there is, as you know, distortion. Here you will actually find dogs that can harm humans. Why? Because you created them that way. In the higher realms, animals speak to you a truth about God's Love for you only. In the higher levels, or the natural Web of Life, animals most certainly do not eat each other's bodies. It is only your terrible distortion of life into lack that has brought about eating at all. Luckily, I'm still embodied here on this most dense level, so I can be more philosophical about such things. And even I'm into eating other animal's bodies. In the journeys beyond time that we all take, it's unimaginable to eat each other's flesh, or ever to bite or scratch or hurt a human being in any way. Since God's original thought was that we are ever and always a blessing to you, that is what we are, unless we are influenced by your creations.

On the higher levels, any time you are in need of reassurance about a certain aspect of your being, an animal appears and "speaks the truth of its being." It speaks its true nature. And thus you will understand what Goddess is saying. Understanding it, we would join in a fun relationship where I would continue to remind you of the message that I am, and then I would disappear. If you loved the message I brought, you could choose to anchor it in your life and we would become wonderful companions. If this is the case, then every time you think of me, I will always be there.

In the condition you are currently in—falling asleep and then waking again and again, we, your companions, seem to be with you in life after life. Really we are simply forever with you.

These thoughts of God that are we, the animals, are pure expressions of an aspect or aspects of God. This is always true. We do not ever change. If you are seeing a distorted image of an animal, this is your imagination. It is your creation within the theater of Time—no more real than any of this. Thus, you can always trust that if you "follow" an animal back to a place of purity of heart, that animal will lead you to God. That animal will teach you the true qualities that were inherent in the thought of God at the time of the animal's creation. Thus we can be very great allies to you.

This fact of the illusions that are laid upon us explains to you why people ultimately have animals that are like them. By looking at someone's animals, you can learn a lot about them—things they are even hiding from themselves.

The threads of Love that are our creation, our connection in the mind of the Creator—it is from these threads, the threads of the lives of all living things, that the Web of Life is made. It is the movements of our existence that weave the Web on every level. And, of course, just like everything else, the Web of Life can be experienced on every level. From the lowest level, the Web is an entangling of sometimes opposing and often confusing energies, all the way to the highest level in which every thread is a completely luminous trail of dancing, singing Light.

O, Follow Me! I will take you dancing on the Web of Life. And as we dance, Creation will be revealed to you. You will be blessed by God/Goddess and you will be held in sacred communion. It is a communion where, reverently, you will touch God's face as you come to full awareness of yourselves—as God's heart.

God is radiant Love.
This Love
is seeking you
every moment
through all eternity.
Unless you consciously
turn away,
God will always
find you.
So, anyone who is not
actively away
from God
will be with God.

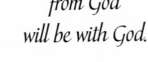

On Death

I am going to speak to you about death. This is a subject that is on your mind often when you look at me. Because I'm what you see as "older," you have fears about "losing me." It is a very good thing that you have a practice of transforming these thoughts. But, it is now in your timing to explore this topic.

First, let me tell you how it looks to a cat. It is nothing to even be concerned about. We are slipping in and out of here continually. We are not at all like humans, for we have not cut ourselves off from the rest of Creation and from the rest of our beings, as humanity has. So to us it is less of a problem than taking off the clothes that you humans wear. You have an image I have seen in your mind that explains it accurately. (Editor's Note: This was a scene in the movie, Cocoon, where the heroine unzips her body and flies in her light body.) This is exactly how death is.

We dance each day on the Web of Life. We see all around us the entrance points to the spiritual world, and we regularly slip through to expand ourselves, to dance and play and resonate with all of our Creator's life.

You have been far too concerned with a limited version–no! a limited version within a limited version!–of the death experience. Something that you read made a negative impression that you must now get beyond. It is all about what you know as your truth. It is not about fleeting fears that arise about death. You know the law–like attracts like. Well this applies more clearly and absolutely than ever if you are in the process of leaving your lower and most cumbersome vehicle. Death truly is about your heart.

The process of dying is a great reunion of the heart. I know this because, being free, I watch it all the time. Remember–there is a reason why cats sleep so much. We are exploring the rest of the Web of Life.

So I often stand back and watch what happens as a person phases out of the incarnated consciousness and phases in to the larger reality. The first thing that I see is the signal of the heart. There is an actual beam of light emanating from the consciousness and there is essentially a vibrational pattern or song from the heart. As these issue forth there is a great magnetic response–a response that simply cannot be avoided. It is through this response that all beings in your sector, your slice of life, are drawn perfectly to you. It is like a vibrational lock and key, with the two parts opening in unison with complementary and interweaving energy patterns.

So what will work best for those of you who are more aware is to look around to see who it is that is drawn to your heart. Now, in this I'm not saying you are preparing for a death experience. Not at all. Just that it will enrich your life to have contact now with your larger family.

However, as you are right now experiencing, these people, or beings, are going to become an ever greater and clearer part of your life. And for those who are climbing into the highest tree branches where you can easily see beyond the veil and into the Web of Life, well, you will simply become like a cat! You will dance across the bridge of Time to play the songs of Love as your feet touch the chords of the great strings of the weaving of the Web of Life.

I can promise you that as you dance forth into the adventure, first you will see beauty, but as if you were in a bit of a fog. Then as the fog clears, your heart will call you to play your song. It's difficult to explain. But once you see yourselves and know yourselves, you will intuitively know how to play the song of your being by the way you move on/in the great tapestry. This song of your being is the most beautiful experience. It is infallible. It describes you absolutely perfectly to all who are a part of this dancing and radiant life. Ah, it is like our communion only far more beautiful and far clearer.

God is radiant Love. This Love is seeking you every moment through all eternity. Unless you consciously turn away, God will always find you. So, anyone who is not actively away from God will be with God. You may want to read this a large number of times until it is fully accepted in your consciousness. So, I hope you see from this that you will never be lost. There can be no negative experiences and nothing can pretend otherwise, unless you actively choose to turn away. Since certainly you have not turned away, God will always find you, commune with you, lift you. God is reaching to you, to know you in joined communion of consciousness, always.

Now shedding the weight of the body is one way to come into this pared-down relationship in which all incorrect interpretations of the consciousness are overcome. But it is also a very viable option to develop the total communion with the truth of life, the great Web of Life, *through* the body so it does not become an obstacle or impediment. This is what God is bringing to you in the things you are learning. If the body becomes a conscious conduit of the connecting Love, it can itself be raised up. It can overcome all limitation, even death.

What you are beginning to learn about the truth of your cells is no accident. As you understand that they are open beings, particles on their own vision quest, then once so recognized, you can essentially shoot the light through the cells and commune directly with the Web of Life. So understanding and including these cells, the little beings, not only dramatically increases your light quotient, it enhances the flow of information between All That Is without and All That Is within, until what you find in the purity of Love, greater Love, without, becomes what is within.

This is a topic we most definitely need to cover from other angles in the future. Thanks for listening.

*Where do you
think animals are
when they sleep
so much?
All of us are
out upon the streams
of sparkling light
that is
the Web of Life.*

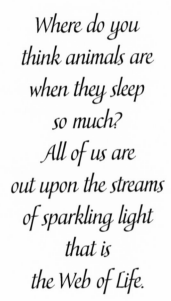

In Her Will

Even a moment visiting together will be helpful—for it is time for us to be in touch regularly and for much of it to be recorded, too. I am ever present when the heart strings of the Web of Life are plucked by the fingers of She who loves us and who holds us in the world. So I listen with eager ears, as if listening for a mouse on a moonlit night.

Yes, of course, death isn't real. Can you possibly think I don't know this? Yet I put on this body here so you could see me, so we could play and learn, for at the time you called me to you there was no way we could relate in only consciousness.

Where do you think animals are when they sleep so much? All of us are out upon the streams of sparkling light that is the Web of Life. Each strand is filled with pearls—like dewdrops on a spider's web in the garden in the morning. And every pearl is a world, a place, a dip or dish or crescendo in the symphony of life. And I can visit everyone! I can dip and taste and splash and glide. I can be greeted in Love by myriads of life and then I can open my eyes and see you in bed, friend of my deepest heart.

We've danced before, of course. Not through lives on Earth, as so many believe we do, but through streams and tunnels of Her laughter, through rainbows of Her beauty—you, together, a being of Love and I your special friend (playmate). But wherever we went and however we loved there was always the knowledge of this world in our hearts until we decided at last that we had to dip in and see how we could serve Her Love and release our brothers and sisters from the prison of their minds.

Now this form I wear seems cumbersome. You are correct. It has been hurting me. So why not make another? What's the point of staying here like this? And if you will track me through my journey, it will create for many another road to life.* For many love me and are waiting for my books, which to me are already out there—for the plan and its fruition exist together in the truth. Since Time is an illusion, I can see how many lonely hearts are opened by our story (which, by the way, must be published soon. Book One can stop with my promise to you of how I will return.)

I'm not averse to a healing, as you call it, but only if these limitations are released. There is something about these bodies where the life force gets constricted in them the longer you use them.

We can switch the story, shifting to another "parallel reality." I'm open to such things. But I yet believe we will serve my friends, all those humans whose hearts I open, by showing them that death is not to be feared, rather than showing it "overcome," which they cannot relate to yet. I am a connecting point to a large ring of opening hearts. I tell you they are waiting for me, and I don't want to disappoint them

Maya** came to show you this–the trajectory of an animal's spirit. But she didn't establish a link as I have to the hearts of human beings. The SoulMate message you bring for God will pour outward from above in concentric rings. My story will touch the waiting hearts on the great middle ring of humanity. Trust me on this–I see it spreading before me now.

So hold me in Love. I'm already with God*–happily lying in the sun of Her Love. I am open to the path I am taking from here. Just know that bodies are a cumbersome spot of inflexible energy–a knot in the Web that it's hard to get past–yes, frozen.

I want to play like a kitten and to be on your bed and to be in communion with you all of the time. If you can help me do this without transferring to another body, so be it! Her Will is mine. My question I leave you with is this. Is your Will in Hers about this, as well? If so, and I'm risen, returned to "kittenhood" and I look and see I wear this same fur, I will rejoice that we accomplished your desire by leaving it all up to the One we both love.

*This message was the first time that Magic Cat told Yael that he might be exchanging his tired body for a new one, and that this event would be a great teaching about death.

**Maya was Yael and Doug's beloved dog who was killed in an accident. After Maya transitioned, Yael

immediately heard her calling, and telling them that she would return soon and where and how. She reappeared as Angel Maya, their current adorable female Pomeranian.

The light
came twinkling on again
when I heard and
felt you promise God
to use the ending of my life
in this form,
my death,
in other words,
to strengthen your belief
in life
and not to reinforce
the seeming reality
and loss of death

Shifting the Patterns of Thinking and Holding onto Life While Facing Death

Thank you for tuning to me, for choosing me as your focus. You are learning more about focus every moment. In this glory of light there are a million streams spreading out from just this moment, from you and me and all the lives we are touching. All you have to do is focus on any strand within the whole and you are there with that being, that consciousness, delighting in another perspective in God.

Today I am floating in this light. I am wrapped in it, and at the same time I am drinking this sweet nectar. It is the nectar of my Love for you. And oh my, it is getting sweeter every moment. This nectar is the nourishment, the precious elixir that comes from the fruit of our experience together. It is this nectar that we shall feed to God's precious ones–those She has brought us here to serve together.

Can you feel the resonance and the power of that word–"together"? And can you feel it growing stronger even as we commune here together? Oh, I can feel it! And my heart rejoices.

Here is what I see when I see "together." I see that yesterday, until you came, I was in a wasteland of wanting you.* I could not have articulated it. And of course we were able to communicate in consciousness. I didn't know it, but I was waiting. Waiting for something I already had been shown, in that inner view, from that One whom I name the Goddess, or Creator.

It wasn't until you made "the choice" that it all came back to me. Oh, but when you did (even before you were fully sure of it yourself), everything changed. It was like I was waiting on a Now point and all the paths that were fanning forth looked wrong somehow, and bleak. Then, suddenly, you were home and everything changed.

What changed was not about the physical homecoming.* It was about the homecoming of the Spirit. And in one moment, the whole pattern upon which I rested changed. And with that change came this sweet remembrance.

So I record it here, for our precious ones, Goddess' tender children whom she holds to her breast. The shift occurred. The pattern moved. The light came twinkling on again when I heard and felt you promise God to use the ending of my life in this form, my death, in other words, to strengthen your belief in life and not to reinforce the seeming reality and loss of death. In that moment many things were revealed to me–promises made, sealed in our hearts–Loves chosen, forms on Earth, to solidify the pattern, set the course.

In that moment, all the rivers of your life came Home to Her as well, and the pattern of light, the streaming paths of possibility upon which I now rest, are supported tenderly with angel song and wrapped in grace.

Thank you. Thank you for coming Home, because what we are to do here is very important. There are choices of such impact that even I, who know these things, cannot say where this will go exactly (this is exciting!). So much energy is building here that it really could explode. I'm preparing for the flash! But what it will reveal when it is done I do not know.

I only know this. I will be with you, embarking on a quest to bring life back to humanity–to resurrect the child of the Goddess–to create a sparkling path so bright that even those who are stumbling along as if blind cannot fail to see it. When the flash comes, will I be regenerated here, in this form, this body? Or will I be a kitten, in a newly formed body, playful, and waiting for you? I do not know. But I do know our work will continue. Instead of work we should say our joy or we could say our exciting service, because this transition from death to life will provide the material for a new book on Christedness, from an animal's point of view.

What this means, my beautiful friend, friend whom I love so very much, friend to whom I will always come, no matter what the time or age in the world of human beings, is this. *Your decision to see and feel and believe in only life even while looking right into the eyes of death will lay a pathway across the world and into the hearts of* *those we serve. **It will turn them to life again.***

Animals know life. We feel it singing in us, both in body and in spirit. I can't wait until I can show you and have you feel this experience. Life speaks to us. Every moment in the life of an animal is full to overflowing with friendship and joy as millions of beings continually share the life they are with us. We do worship life. We breathe every breath in living praise for this most incredible gift. To be alive! To be filled up with life. To feel its eternal nature forever washing through us, just as blood flows through a physical body. Every moment is a celebration of life. Even more, we have a deep deep deep gratitude for the gift. The knowledge that forms here may shift but the life that animates them is our eternal gift.

The fact that you have now been able to take all the proof of death's "reality," especially the "loss" of your beloved child,** and shift your focus to only life–oh, it is a miracle! A miracle of consciousness, of remembering the truth and the vows that we made–to open up the glorious experience of eternal life for humanity through the help of animals, for whom it is so immanent, so real, so full, so glorious.

It amazes us that human beings can turn away from life–that they can "shut it down" and can label it as ending. And most shocking of all that millions of you can seek annihilation every single day that you're alive. Oh, can you feel my disbelief? How could you, any of you, take the greatest gift of our Creator and spurn it. Oh, I'm speechless, for to do such a thing is really to spit in the face of God. It makes my head spin and makes my body feel ill. I believe I'd better turn away from such considerations. Yet perhaps you can see that if even a moment of contemplating the spurning of life makes me feel ill in both body and spirit, what does it do to humans? It creates the world you see. And it creates a world full of sickness from focusing on such things.

Animals do not live in the same world as humans. We live in a world of life, even though we live right here beside you. Even when our bodies die, when we are hurt and maimed by human beings, our focus ever lives in the great and glorious living Web of Life.

We are streams of Love that God has sent to you, humanity. We are messages from your greater selves as well. Every animal comes with a message, and the things our bodies seem to do are a reflection of your consciousness in its present state. In many ways we are like a perfect mirror. Our light is so bright and our Love is so pure and it literally shines so brilliantly that you can see consensual reality as it lives in you reflected back by the shining surface of our consciousness, our Love. As you move beyond any limitation of life (by your beliefs) then truly we will reflect back to you forms that do not die. And those who are just waking to Love will find each animal that comes into their lives is more loving and more beautiful than the ones before.

You and I have been deep and powerful friends, our relationship evolving as your consciousness awakened here. As you remembered more and more the truth of Love, then our consciousness could blend and speak and our giving could evolve from this. This is the true way of things. If Love is the focus and really is, not some secret purpose of human ego, the only result is giving. We give to others the elixir of life that is generated by a loving union, be it friendship or SoulMate-type of Love.

By this you can see revealed the reflection of human consciousness in the animals–that they compete with each other and fight and even kill. This is NOT the truth of us. This is human beings looking in the mirror of our hearts, our lives. It is very potent.

Thank you. Can you feel what is happening here? Can you feel the opening of our Love into a great and fragrant flower that we will present, for Her, to others (to all of humankind if our favorite pattern comes to pass!). How different this is from Orange Kitty!*** That you can now affirm your deep belief in God, in life, while looking at my body die–oh, let this speak to you! And just in case you don't get the message, I will give it to you.

You are "walking back" the greatest symbol of the lie –that which is called anti-Christ itself. It is death. For if God is Love exploding forth as life and only life, what greater symbol of reversal could there be than death? And if you cannot ever be separate from God (which you cannot), then you cannot be separate from life.

As She has said to you, death is the great pretender. It is the lie of death which causes people to turn away from life. Of course - why focus on life when all it will lead to is death? Well I can tell you that nothing is farther from the truth. And what it takes to heal it (this terrible dream, this nightmare–I use the concept from your mind because rather than dreaming when I'm "asleep," I'm dancing forth out on the Web of Life)… Anyway, for you to use my death to deepen your commitment to life–this is it! This is what it takes! And the next body will reflect this, the next form that I wear. And of course as you continue to shift back to life, then all bodies in your family will reflect this glorious living light in which we are alive forever.

You know that right now death does still have a hold in your consciousness, your heart's beliefs. No matter how much you don't want it to, it is there. There are thoughts that rise up, carrying shadows on them and traces of a past experience of great pain—the pain of "losing" one whom you loved. This is swiftly changing but, in honesty, you know it isn't here yet.

So my body seems to die. My spirit will come back wearing another one. But for me, nothing changes. I am here with you. That's it. I'm here with you. All the rest is like flickering shadows brought forth by the light of a blazing campfire. Without the light you wouldn't even see the shadows. In other words, those who have no light can't see the shadows dancing, can't make out that they have shape and can be noticed. All they see is inky blackness of an uninterrupted night.

Shall we go forth to point to life, unlimited and glorious? I want to assist you (and thus to show so many others) to see how you must love life, must cherish it, must actively remember our Creator's precious gift to us. We must continually give thanks to Her for every precious moment. We must notice life (as She has told you) for where your focus rests is ever what you amplify–what you create more of.

In closing, may I say to you that I am truly wanting to "hang out" with you. I want you to hold my failing body while I reach to you in consciousness and help you to affirm that even though you look at death–hold it in your arms, in fact–nothing really dies. Certainly not me. I'll be back with you in an instant from my point of view. Certainly it will not be long if it's kitten that comes through to you which is what I still suspect.

Please record your feelings, your decisions, as well as our communion. This is important! Record the times of grief as well as the sweet triumph of the moments where you can see right through death's mask upon my face. Hold me, if you can, when I transition. Hold me for sure in spirit (consciousness) if you cannot in body. I have no idea how it will go or if I'll have any control. I do know that what I wish to do is "beam" to you the truth of me, alive–alive eternally even at the moment that death seems to have me.

Focus on life–everywhere in everything. Oh, rejoice in it and celebrate it everywhere! In this consensual reality you are programmed out of exuberance. You are taught not to feel joyful for no reason (and, of course, the ego never finds a reason good enough!).

Animals are going to be (are is the word I want to use) instrumental in the opening of human beings back to Love. Just like you, we're in place, as all of Nature is, to rock you, cajole you and jolt you back to only life.

One last note–the concept of aging is one of the ways that life is limited by human beings. It's gotta go. For you and for all your animals. It may take a while before it's really gone. Be patient with yourselves. And as our Creator shows me now, do not ever judge each other if one takes a little longer to get something. She says to remind you that the one taking longer may be the one doing the greater service by laying the path for the others following.

LIFE! Come share it with me. Come Home as soon as you can. I'm waiting to be with you "in body" and in consciousness because the pattern now available to us fits the one She shows me that we are meant to be together, for the world.

Your Magic Cat

PS –Don't change my name if I change my form. It's still me!

Yael and Doug had just returned from camping at the lake when Magic Cat began his transition out of his body.

**Yael had a son seventeen years ago who at 15 months of age suddenly became ill and made his transition. This event caused a rift in Yael's deep Love of God that was only healed as she began to understand the truth that there is no "death."*

***Orange Kitty was another animal of Yael's who experienced a long and painful death. It was an excruciating passage for Yael.

Just as you become
available to your SoulMate
in proportion to your open heart,
so too will your openness
be reflected by us –
so you will see animals
reflected two-by-two.
They will appear in pairs
as in the time of Noah –
a positive and a negative
always seen together.
Animals will soon be
mating for life,
as the beautiful vibration
of your Twin Flame Love
becomes manifest in us.

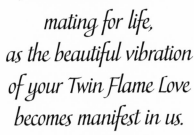

The Symbols of the World Change
As We Change Our Consciousness

Yes, I am here with you, to bring you joy and sweet release from your sadness, because I am free. I'm flying forth, bounding through the Web of Life, coming close to touch and taste the Earth. It is as if the Earth is one great catnip ball and I am mad with pleasure as I roll and tumble until I can't tell where I begin or end. You must feel joy like this! It is joy so great that joy is the only thing you are. Not cat, not person, not stream of light, and certainly not body. Pure joy so profound that Now is swallowed in it.

This is the truth of my life. It is the truth of what I bring to you as gifts–and the truth that the mirror of this body I now leave (discard) contained the reflections of your older heart beliefs. I was a stray, lost and starving, when I came to your door because I reflected the inner core of you. The core of you at that time was yet a child crying for her nourishment, lost within her humanness and her belief in pain and loss.

Of course you never thought of this because it's what I'm here to show you! So if you grasped it by yourself, what would there be for me to do? And yes, Christos* likewise, does mirror your belief in pain. And yet, having said this, let me remind you that this is Her work we do. So everything you hold within is that which you have purposefully, at Her request, come to bring back Home to Love. And we, of course, your animals, absolutely are here to do this with you.

Thus, as I return, now that you have chosen not to be your humanness but to cling to life no matter what you see reflected all around you, your reflections will change. (The things around you reflect you on the mirror of their consciousness.) The most powerful of these for you, of course, are the animals.

So my new body will reflect these things—the joy and exuberance of life and the tender communion of inclusiveness, of family. There will be a place for me at your head as you sleep. And together we'll make harmony among all the animals. I will come to you in a pampered body, pedigreed and beautiful. And I will come to you with my mate, my SoulMate if you will.**

Yes, you heard this right! So you begin to see exactly how this reflection process works. You do not need to feel badly that you aren't rescuing a kitten from the pound, because that would not reflect you. Do you see? You have nothing left in you that is abandoned and "on the edge," barely sure if you will live or die. And you are realizing that you don't have to rescue anyone from death. Death is not a part of life in the Real Web. Ah, so I will come to you fat and sassy, completely loved, pampered to the best of the ability of the breeders. And I will have a littermate, a **her** that I'll come with. And we shall mirror forth the New World you're building here.

I showed you yesterday, though all the world's a stage, the characters, the costumes, the symbols that the player's wear (that which we call bodies) and the situations in these lives will reflect the change in consciousness. They will essentially be showing you how far you've come and what have become your heart's assurances. Especially the animals, for we are crystal consciousness upon which your heart's beliefs reflect.

Thus shall the natural world very precisely change to mirror the shifts in consciousness that human beings make. As they leave behind their "humanness" (as you have been doing so beautifully), everything in the world will show forth the truth of Love rather than the truth of Love and anti-Love. One truth–that God is ONLY Love, not Love and "something else" that is not Love. Is it not strange that so many animals, especially in this country, the enlightened society, are put to death? That right there shows you how deeply human beings believe in death instead of choosing life.

Even the New World is a symbol. You know this, of course, because it has forever already existed in God as perfection. But the New World is a progression of the symbols that are your life on Earth. And thus you will now get to see the lion lying with the lamb, and Nature will reveal to you that truth of every twig. Every moth and butterfly. Everything as it reflects to you your consciousness as a Child of Our Creator.

Just as you become available to your SoulMate in proportion to your open heart, so too will your openness be reflected by us—so you will see animals reflected two-by-two. They will appear in pairs as in the time of Noah—a positive and a negative always seen together. Animals will soon be mating for life, as the beautiful vibration of your Twin Flame Love becomes manifest in us. Thus shall this world accurately reflect the progression of human consciousness made manifest before you. Isn't this exciting?

It will move closer and closer to perfection. The symbols of negativity will vanish, disappear. The New World will be born, but you must remember that New World is a symbol. It is a bridge, until, at last, the world as you know it will be gone, because the only thing in your consciousness will be Love and nothing else. Then bodies and stories and history will cease and you will be here, on the Web of Life with me.

I'm right here. Do you feel this light? You have been seeing light around my body because you and I connect there, when you are looking at it. We connect because you reach out in consciousness to me because you are not "buying it," that this body is me before you. You also see the light of all the angels in attendance.

Release me from the body. You did hear me correctly. We have no more need of it, you or I. If you think that you do, you can read this message over, or come to me in spirit and I will reassure you. Yes, we have been wonderful friends using that body as our meeting point for consciousness. But our friendship goes far beyond this

Time or Place. You called me to you when you had gained enough consciousness to remember me and to remember that all you had to do was call me and I would be there.

The body has its own consciousness. It continues on with a steadfast pursuit of life that is beyond reason. This clinging to life is the vestiges of fear imprinted upon, or in, the body as it was created to begin with. It was created, balanced between life and death and perceiving its times as a struggle between the two. The body seeks life because it also fears death. This is the fact of the vibrational resonance of which it is made. So the body continues "mindlessly" to "fight death" until there is no energy left and it has to succumb—to release the rigid form in which it has held itself—and to become energy once again. Only when this happens is the tie to the consciousness inhabiting the body completely severed or released.

You will know from what I show you today how successfully you have walked this course, the one called "choosing life." For the record, you have also freed all the energy you had tied up in "the mother's response" or the human response to your son's death.*** Also for the record —when you saw yourself standing on that very same crossroad, connected to the spirit [of your son] so beautifully that you knew death is an illusion but, seeing his dying body, you made the choice to feel your human pain. And right there, with Joshua, your son, began twenty-seven years of humanness where his death is concerned. Twenty-seven years of fear and of the belief in loss. It happened because you couldn't stand strong in your spirit, where you had been shown and had experienced the truth firsthand of his living presence. You do know now that you had to make the choice you did in order to feel the human side, so that you could lay a path for others. Only now do you understand that this path is across the great divide of death.

Yet this time, standing in tears with my body, when the same choice appeared before you, you remembered. So you chose the other path today. You chose not to allow your humanness. And with that choice you set me free. Not that I am not free on my own, but I agreed to create this path with you. It is this that we must write about and place it under Animal Communication on the internet. Please do this right away. I would love to have something up before I "leave." And I want to release the body.****

Here's how you can help me. Sit together, you of my family here, creating your SoulMate heart as a place of peace and refuge for those beings that are my body. Soak my body in the light, the river that flows through your Twin Flame hearts. Reassure every cell and corpuscle, every fiber and every nerve that there is only life. Show them through your SoulMate hearts the truth of their existence–that they are being freed to come to live in Love. Let us see if this will work. I will be assisting, for I can now communicate with every cell from only light, from that place of Love's extended field–that is larger than the cosmos that you can yet perceive.

I know our agreement. I believe my body is fast approaching a time where its discomfort will begin to be expressed. When the Master did this, the whole sky darkened and the Earth shuddered and rumbled–such was the power of a body touched by Christos (Jesus, not our dog of the same name!).

You have made your choices, the ones that Our Creator hoped that you would make–to choose life while looking at death, the symbol of belief in anti-life, in separation from God. This you have done well, and it is the beginning of your blossoming into your greater work. And you chose not to allow your human self to take over. You have no idea how great an accomplishment this is! Especially with all those years of carrying the mother's pain, your humanness. That has a very big pull on you to follow it again. It had been such a part of you, but you refused it. And I rejoice!

The needle would be okay. I am not that body! And those are living beings within it, trapped in anguish. It is only streams of anti-Love that have those cell consciousnesses reversed. There is a community in this/that body. One that can be freed just as you are here to free humanity from a consciousness reversed. Let's sleep together more today. As we lay there, bodies side-by-side, we can commune in the spirit in the freedom of our Love. Let us honor and do service to the steams of consciousness manifesting now as the body that I wore.

Please send a letter to your/my people, all of them, telling them of my "passing," of my shift in vehicles, and asking for their prayers to life, as well as telling them that the story of this "passing" will soon be up online. How do I, a cat, converse about such things? I show to you the lines of our service, the path on which we agreed and you, if you are open, know what it means in terms of our world as it is now. So I think of our service and you receive the symbol of the "internet." Anyway, I want to have something in their hands/hearts before I completely disconnect from this body all the way. Then we can continue, but the initial contact with everyone surrounding us (the whole list) must be made now–tonight. I know you won't mind. This will connect their heart to me and make them connected to our further adventures.****

We may be able to accomplish this with prayer, with loving the cells free of the pull of anti-Love. It is only an appearance, this is true–but somebody's consciousness has been supporting it. Remember that human beings are creators and that consciousness is the real truth of life. It is also, when it is reversed, the truth of anti-life. So just as an embodiment of consciousness (Lucifer) supports the space in which you manifest your dream, just so do you convince (or commandeer) other streams of consciousness to manifest this play of Love and anti-Love.

Nothing is Real but Love, but a lot of beings believe that anti-Love is real. It's not that this changes anything because the answer is still the same, always the same. Everything is made right by Love. So even the frozen Love (which is really frozen consciousness) that manifests this world must be freed by being melted with Love. So the answer to all things frozen or reversed is to pour Love through them through your SoulMate heart. When this becomes the only thing you do, any frozen energies, anything reversed is simply magnetized to Love in your presence. I only mention the body's cells so you will have compassion and fill every one with Love. Do only this and all else is free, released, to be only the Love it is.

I am your friend always and forever. You will see!
And any friend of yours simply has to be in service, which
I assure you is the truth for me.

*Christos is Yael's beloved Pomeranian who began to
show signs of painful arthritis in the past few years.

**For the story of Magic Cat's arrival in his beautiful
new pedigreed Rag Doll body with his SoulMate, Magic's
Love, see The Story of Magic Cat at the beginning of the book
and the pictures in the center of the book.

***See the footnote in the previous message.

****The story of Magic's release of his body and Magic's
messages were placed on our website, _www.circleoflight.net_, per
his request. We, his family, gently held his physical body and
placed him in our hearts as he easily transitioned.

Only by pretending to be solid
can you believe at all
that life does not
weave all equally
and flow through
everyone together.
Yet, saying this,
of course you know that
every special container
of consciousness
is cherished by the Goddess.
And each is more precious
than you can believe.
So precious that
we are cherished for eternity.

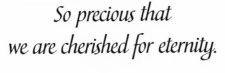

Our Co-Creation of Nature and the Reflections in the "Pond of the World"

Can you see this glorious Creation, filled with streams of living color, each a conscious life? Can you feel also how the sweep of Love comes washing through us, every one, again and again and again? Waves of most exquisite joy, floodlight beams of ecstasy. They light every single life with Her of whom we are all a part.

So we feel Her, know Her, rock within the waves of Her love. Each of us aware, yet every one a container of the same One, same Love, same grace. So when I come to you, my precious friend, please do not feel that it is "either God/Goddess or Magic Cat speaking today." It is both. For I am transparent–as are we all, and Her Love is obvious in me, held only in the container of light that is my consciousness. It is, I might add, a container that is completely permeable, as are you. So it cannot ever be "either God or one of us." Not ever. Because whomever you feel, whomever you bring into the focus of your consciousness, every one is filled with God/Goddess as well.

Only by pretending to be solid can you believe at all that life does not weave all equally and flow through everyone together. Yet, saying this, of course you know that every special container of consciousness is cherished by the Goddess. And each is more precious than you can believe. So precious that we are cherished for eternity.

So when I come to you now, She comes to you as well, using the window of my consciousness to show you a new perspective than the one you have as you. And this is what life is, what Creation is, of course - each of us showing the others a unique perspective of the Creator.

She is Mother to me because like a mother cat she cares for me, feeds me and cherishes me. And like a kitten I am ever resting in the shelter of Her heart.

You are an animal communicator. Not one who does little snips of life in the physical, but one with the capacity to reveal these magnificent truths, of how Real Love is, how present, how filled with Her, and most of all how resplendent is Her message. She can say Love in trillions upon trillions of ways. Each one is a life. Each one is a precious vessel, a container of Her Love. Each one is a ribbon of light awash across the universe, adornment for Her in her endless and ecstatic life.

Every life expresses Her beauty. Just as a physical woman adorns her body, She of whom we are made wears strings of pearls that are great beings, and she wears the rainbows of our consciousnesses as we are woven together in our Love for Her.

Every time I come to you, you have to remember that all life is transparent to God/Goddess, meaning that each and every being is a container made of consciousness through which Goddess' loving presence flows without impediment. So–no more of this "Magic or God" stuff in you! We are both–especially animals. For even here upon the Earth we are completely filled with Her Love, packaged very carefully that Her Love might have access to the human heart through us.

So let me tell you a little bit about how I am now. Notice that I didn't say "where" I am, because where is certainly irrelevant from here. How I am is flooded with the ecstatic glory of all of life. I am feeling it all - the magnificence, the joyousness, the waves of Love that are lifting me every moment that is ever Now. And I am filled to overflowing with the messages of Love that are the world. I see the world. I see life on Earth exactly as you might see a reflection on a pond. And it is so incredible. How She does this! How She knows you so well, so perfectly. So well that, spread out before you in the most delicious jewel tones, is "life in Nature" as it appears on Earth.

She has taken every stream of life and made from it an image. An image that speaks perfectly of the essence of that life. So I feel and know in my heart this amazing Love for every beautiful stream of life, alive and ever present in this that is Real Life. And feeling it, absorbing it, drinking in its truth as Love, then I see a place where the "life on Earth" begins. It is a shimmering oasis in the middle of a field of dancing streams of light and conscious identities as Love. Reflected in the "pond" of life on Earth I see trees and mountains and meadows filled with flowers and with grass. I see the pictures we have made, under God's advisory, that show forth the reflection of that which grows and lives in Goddess.

So I experience both. The streams of luminous consciousness with which She fills each moment always, and that oasis that is the "pond" upon which we are reflected as life on Earth. You are fast approaching this point of view as well—where you will gasp in wonder at the fabulous reflections that we have created in Her to represent the life we are. And as your ability grows to feel and know the spirit (or the life as consciousness) as well as the reflection here of what each really is, you will finally be present at the Moment of Creation. For in each pulse the Love streams forth, filling every container of consciousness alive and then reflecting in an image, that very life upon the "pond" of the world.

My message for today is that She is always shining through me, and when we commune, you can trust that She is always speaking through me. Only through the human mind is the transparency of life refused. And of course humans are merely turned away, pretending to be solid instead of transparent. Because if She were really refused, life would cease - which it will not.

So, the first message from us to you is that if you are truly in service to Love, then you are transparent, too. She shines through you. And so do we, all the life She has made. You must allow all natural life, all glorious streams of Her embodiment, all the great spotlights of the angels' Love to shine through you to Earth. You must now expand your definitions of God. We need you. We, this great and glorious, sparkling kaleidoscope of life that She is, each of us alive in Her. And in ways you don't comprehend yet, we also are a part of you, for you create with Her, and we all reflect your relationship with Her in every way. How can I explain this?

You, a Twin Flame stream exploring Her in whom you live and whom you love, notice a certain relationship you have with Her. With a spark, that recognition becomes a stream of life. It is a stream created in the union of you and Her, and it is given life by the joined consciousness of you and the Creator. So these lives are "in you." They are also "in Her." They become the embodiment of a specific piece of your relationship with Her.

These different streams, when reflected in the "pond" of life on Earth, are seen by you as every form of beauty and joy and glory and life. Unfortunately, your split-consciousness at present, also imagines an "opposite" form that you think must exist because you believe in light and dark. But the dark is just imagined.

So just as you can feel the truth of each other and of Goddess, so you can also discern what part of your relationship with our Creator each element of natural beauty represents. So what you see as Nature is Real life, Her life, embodied in consciousness. Yet you are co-creators. The real stream of consciousness behind the symbols, each one, can tell you about another facet of your co-creatorship and your relationship with Her. This is why She has called it a set of symbols by which She speaks to you. What She speaks of, then, is your relationship and all the many streams of life co-created by it.

If you give voice through you to Nature, then human beings will gain much understanding of their relationship with Goddess/God.

All of life can speak through you exactly as She does. And I promise you that you are completely in your Love. You will not be fooled by duality a bit. Humanity is hungry for this feeling of life's unity, and how they long to feel and know the beauty of the natural world. Oh, from my current vantage point (talk about the catbird seat!), I can feel how sick they are (literally) of the world of lies and pain they see. Every message of Nature's beauty, of the sweet support and Love of life itself is like administering lifesaving measures to one who is very ill. For ill they are. They have "driven themselves from paradise" into a truly horrible world. Any glimpse of paradise you give them is soul food, literally, without which they shall become more "sick at heart."

Now, as for me. We are definitely entering the phase of service together (as is everyone in your life). When I return, I will be in a refined body and a refined state, "bent on service." I must be very beautiful because my picture (and my SoulMate's) will be everywhere. I shall be the "spokesmodel" for animal communication and for SoulMates to the general population. Wait and see!

So—I feel that a Himalayan body would be perfect. Because everyone who sees me and especially the two of us together will be affected right away. You just need to see a Seal Point and your mind will change. Oh—blue eyes will work great! However, I'm willing to negotiate with your tastes (you created those images, I merely sent you the "impression" called "cat body"). Nonetheless, you have to remember I must have a body that is beautiful (breathtaking would be good!). Long-haired and pampered.

Keep your thoughts away from strays. (No more thoughts of the shelter. There can be NO negative experiences!) I will happily consider other Persian bodies, or other bodies that can promise beauty genetically. I can work with personality and vibration but there is both instinct and genetics to consider too because, like you, I'm connecting to the animals here within the world. Consequently, please be aware that you will have parts to play in socializing the "instinctual kitty" in my new package.*

This will be fun! This can also be a unifying endeavor. You can ask my people (given my needed qualities of beauty, pampered-ness and health) what recommendations they might have for a "type" of cat for my new body! After all, I will be their spokesmodel. (A big cat grin!) And keep me in your glorious hearts as we "prepare the mold" and make it happen. Yes, I can work with bodies already appearing in form, but they must be young kittens, weaning age and no more, because early contact with you is important.

I hope you will embark on this with a spirit of adventure. I have "high-priority" in the animal world, so any cat would be thrilled to be a part of this. Do not miss me! Instead, turn and make contact, just as you did today. Let's go look at kitty pictures, shall we?

*And as you already know, Magic Cat returned on October 24, 2003 as a gorgeous Rag Doll cat.

To The Reader

If you have resonated strongly with what you have just read, we invite you to explore the other books in the Say "Yes" to Love Series, listed at the front of this volume. We also invite you to visit our active Circle of Light website , www.circleoflight.net, where we have an Animal Communication page and more messages from Magic Cat posted.

There you will find the Messages from God that are the subject of our other books. Please also explore our extensive page of readers' questions with answers that elaborate upon the content of the Messages. There is a Sharing from the Heart page; a SoulMate page with stories of SoulMate reunions, and many other features.

You may also join our bi-monthly email list to receive the Messages from God by email and if you wish, our Tuesday Circle mailing list to receive weekly meditations.

May you live with an open heart in a world of Love every moment.

The Team at Circle of Light

A Note from the Editor

I met Yael and Doug Powell on July 17th, 2001, Yael's birthday. God led me right to them through a series of amazingly synchronous events. Because of her disability, Yael rarely leaves her home in Eureka Springs but she and Doug had decided very spontaneously to celebrate her birthday at the home of a close friend in Fayetteville, more than an hour away. That friend had also graciously agreed to host me, a complete stranger, for a few days, while I explored the Fayetteville, AR area, an exploration that I was doing at God's prompting, though I knew not why!

As I sat with Yael and Doug that evening, I was fascinated by their obvious living Love for each other, a Love that pervaded their every word and movement. I learned about Yael's constant pain from a genetic disease of the spine that severely limits her movement, and about Circle of Light, their spiritual center in Eureka Springs. Following dinner Yael read one of the "Messages from God" that have come through her during thirty years of daily meditation. I felt indescribable excitement and upliftment from the extraordinary vibration created and the amazing information of this Message.

We quickly recognized ourselves as the ancient soul family we are, and spent two bliss filled days together at Circle of Light, reconnecting, sharing our lives and our spiritual journeys. Our coming together was divinely guided, step-by-step. Yael and Doug showed me (then) fifty, (now seventy-eight), hand-written notebooks of Messages from God! I committed myself on the spot to utilizing my writing, editing and organizational skills to help them bring this illuminated and needed material out into the world. Our first joint publication effort, **Say "Yes" to Love, God Explains SoulMates**, was accomplished from a distance. Just before Christmas 2001 I took up residence in my new home at Circle of Light Spiritual Center with my spirit family.

After my arrival our "training" began in earnest. The daily Messages intensified, many with specific personal directives for each of us. We all experienced a series of great shifts in consciousness that are ongoing. Within a few months we had the entire content of two more books in the **Say "Yes" to Love** series, **God Unveils SoulMate Love and Sacred Sexuality,** as well as **God's Guidance to LightWorkers**. Since that time our inner training has been directed to what God has called "approaching and accepting Christ consciousness" –clearing the ego, opening the heart and learning the difference between life in the illusion and life in the Real. As quickly as we absorb what is being taught, the material is edited to be outgoing to humanity, much of it through our bi-monthly email list and our Tuesday Circle (see website). With humility and honor, we accept our roles as conduits. Thus, the fourth book in the **Say "Yes"** series, **God Leads Humanity Toward Christ Consciousness** was published, and its companion, **Giving Birth to the Christ Light**, will follow this exciting volume from Magic Cat.

Life at Circle of Light is a series of miracles. The natural beauty of Beaver Lake, the mountains and surrounding woods create a vibration of the New World. The evening sunsets are other-worldly. We watch in awe. Every day Yael meditates several hours, bringing through the amazing teachings from God. The highlight of each day is reading the new Message together. I assist in managing our active wedding business, compiling and editing Messages, directing the growing communication from our website, www.circleoflight.net, writing articles and composing music, helping with practical life necessities and tending the organic garden.

Of course the Circle of Light animals play a large part in my life. You can imagine my shock one very early morning after my arrival when five or six incredible yowls awakened me and in fact shook the whole house. It used to be Magic's habit (in his former body) to let his energy loose in this way now and then at the most unanticipated times. When this occurred it was always followed by five to ten minutes of dog barking. I came to love Magic and his strong personality, and actually sat with him during a large part of his transition, since he (probably purposefully) chose to begin to exit from his former body while Yael and Doug were away camping at the lake.

Now that Magic has returned in his beautiful new body with his darling SoulMate, Magic's Love, I also have the incredible joy of having my very own pet, their sister (littermate), Sweetheart. This is the most intimate experience I have had with an animal and it has changed my life in indescribable ways. My Sweetie follows me everywhere and is the source of much mirth and joy for all of us.

At Circle of Light I have been given the gift of gifts–the joyous feeling of knowing I am in the right place at the right time, with my spirit family, doing the tasks for which I have long been prepared and for which I came into embodiment. I have never been happier! Our commitment as a spiritual family is to bring God's Message of Love forth to our brothers and sisters.

Shanna Mac Lean

A Letter From God to Humanity On Creating A World Of Love

Through Yael and Doug Powell
February 25, 2003

My beloved ones, humanity, I pour this to you with My tender Love, upon streams of light, to touch your waiting hearts. With it come the keys to your remembrance. The remembrance of your beauty and of all the ways I made you in My image. And remembrance of the truth of Love, how every human heart was born in Love and every human being is a child of God. And the remembrance that your heart is our connection and that through it lives your co-creative power. Through it comes your treasure; all the gifts I give to you forever. Through it you will now remember and find yourselves awaking to the truth of Love you are.

How I love you! You are truly the greatest of all miracles. You are My own heart, alive and in embodiment, ready to expand, to ever go forth to give the Love you are. You make Love vibrant, surprising, new. Only you, beloved ones, My precious glorious children, only you can go forth in breathless anticipation and see the Love I Am with a new perspective. Have you not marveled at your wonderful curiosity? At how insatiably you go forward to meet and greet the world? And how deeply you are moved by every expansion of beauty? This is the miracle of your co-creative heart.

My Will for you, all of you, every sweet magnificent golden child of God, is a world of peace and a life of plenty. By looking at Me, you can have these things.

Your heart is the source of your power, your treasure, your identity, your life. Your heart is connected to Me forever. And through your heart you will receive your blessings, the treasures of joy and Love and ever greater abundance that I have waiting for you. Oh! It is My heart's true desire to deliver to you the very keys to heaven that you may live heaven here on Earth, yes, and everywhere you are for all eternity. All that is necessary is for you to return to your heart to find the joy in life that contains the heart's true resonance and the cornucopia of every good, which shall pour forth before you as your life and your world.

I Am a God of Love, dear ones. Forever and forever. There is nothing but Love in Me. Let your heart stir in its remembrance of the great truth, for on it rests the salvation of this precious world and your thousand years of peace that, truly, goes on forever. You have known this, somewhere deep inside. You have known that I Am Love and that all of this before you did not make sense. All the wars and illnesses, the brothers turning upon their brothers, the poverty, the pain, even ageing and death.

Oh, dear ones, I have heard you as you cried out in the dark night of your soul for answers. How every single one of you has asked the question, "If God loves us, why would God create children who have cancer and whole peoples who are starving; so emaciated they already look like skeletons?" It did not seem right to you. This, dear ones, was the message of your heart seeking to show you the truth. And when you have asked, "God, what is my purpose, the meaning of my life?" you have been responding to the nudging of your heart. But some, not hearing their hearts, have turned away, believing I could not be a loving parent to My children if I created such a world of horrors.

Now it is time for the truth. You are ready. And for those of you who read this and already know this, I ask you to deepen your commitment to the living of it, and to pass this on to My other precious children. For those of you who read this and find it inconceivable, I ask you to drop into a focus on your heart for a moment and just allow this to be a possibility. Then pass it on to others–that each hand, each set of eyes, each heart that comes in contact with this letter written in light may also take a moment to allow this possibility to be planted in their life.

Beloved ones, I love you. I love you with a Love as great as the very cosmos. I love you with a joy in your existence that pours forth greater in every moment. I love you as the very heart within Me. I love you, and My Love never wavers, never changes, never ever stops. I long for you to know this, to feel our sweet communion. I long to lay before you all the treasures of creation. You are Mine. Now. And Now. Forever. And nothing can ever change this. It is a fact of your existence.

I did not create this world of pain. You did. You did this when you chose to believe in good, in Love, **and** in something else, which you named the opposite of Love.

271

Call it the moment in the Garden when you ate the fruit of good and evil. Call it the first judgment. Whatever you call it, beloved ones, it is your own creation. And you set yourselves up as being able to decide which was which and thus began this world of duality, of light *and* dark, of Love and anti-Love. But, precious humanity, I Am only Love. And living in Me, you, too, are only Love. So you had to create a false world, a pretend place where darkness could exist, because it cannot exist in that which is ever and only light, which I Am.

You have wandered in the desert of your co-creative minds ever since. For if your heart, connected to Me, knows the truth of only Love, then you had to find another way to view a dual scenario—and thus evolved the tool of your minds.

Oh, dear ones, I do not intend to go into lengthy explanations. All I come to say to you is that you are only Love. And that the more you choose to live through your heart, the more and more clearly you'll see the world as it really is. The more you will experience that true Love of God, the Love that I hold you in each and every moment.

Today you live in a world on the brink of war, a world filled with negativity and so much pain that you have to numb yourselves to survive. So you have nothing to lose by putting to the test what I now show you:

If you know that I Am only Love, then you must know that I Am ever holding for you the world of your inheritance, the world of joyous ecstasy and glorious abundance. You know that I Am not a power you can call on for overcoming darkness, for darkness is not in Me. You know that any moment you connect with Me you connect with the Love and perfection I have always held for you and always will. I Am unchanging Love. In the truth of this Love there is no negativity.

Then what about this world of pain before you? What of the wars and rumors of wars? What of the fear and all the experiences that keep happening in your life? They are you, dreaming, beloved one. They are you lost within the million threads of possibility streaming from your decision to believe in good *and* evil. And just as you dream in the night and your dreams feel real, so it is with this world. So very real and filled with pain, it feels.

There is another way to live. It is to stand before this world of lies each morning and to choose to live in only Love. To consciously reject the illusion of the judgment that there is good and evil. To place your Will in Mine and ask that I lift you up enough that you can see the difference. The difference between the truth of Love that lives within your heart and this world of swirling negativity that is alive within your mind

And once you know that I Am Love and you are ever alive in Me, then you shall truly walk through this world in peace. When you know your home is Me and you affirm the heart, you could walk through a war-torn countryside with bombs falling all around you and know that none could touch you, and none would touch our home.

I will answer your questions. "What about the others?" your heart cries out. "What good is it if I am safe in you, God, if all around me people are in misery?" Beloved ones, the answer is this: as you clear the dream, as you return your Will to Me, as you walk within the truth of the Love we are together, then around you there becomes an aura of peace; a great ball of light comes forth as the living truth of Love you are becoming. At first it may only clear *your* life of the illusion, as your faith in Love restores you to the heaven you belong in, and as, choice-by-choice and day-by-day, you turn to Me for your identity and not to the world you have believed is outside of you. But every day that light grows–exactly as would happen if you turn on a physical light in a dark closet full of scary shapes. The light fills every space–there is no darkness left–and everything that seemed to be so menacing becomes something neutral. Something you can change by moving out the old furniture, or something that you   at least know is harmless.

Thus, as you grow in your ability to stay attuned to Me, to choose the world that is your birthright as a child of God, the greater the circumference of the light that surrounds you. First it begins to light up your neighbors. Suddenly they can see that there are no terrifying things lurking in their lives; that they are free to choose to be happy, to have joy. And with every moment that you spend in communion with the truth of your heart, the greater is that light of truth around you…until you affect the neighborhood and then the town you live in, and the county, then the state in which you live. Until ultimately you will do as Jesus did: everywhere you are, people will see their truth as Love, and knowing this with all their heart they will leave their illnesses, their problems and their strife behind—simply from experiencing the power of your light as you live your life as only Love.

Then as others do the same, soon you'll walk into the world and the illusion of negativity will have to fall away. You will have "turned on the light in the theater," that which you call the world, and all who had believed life was a battle will suddenly be freed.

In your Western world, there is a passage in the Bible from he who came to show you the way to the heart's truth: "You cannot serve both God and mammon." This is exactly what it means. You cannot believe in a world of good and evil and also seek to create a life of Love. For from within the dream of duality every choice for Love contains its opposite.

Beloved ones, if this speaks to you, if something stirs within your heart (or, of course, if you cry out, "Oh, I know this!"), then you are here to show the way. Here to see My face, My Love, in every human being, no matter the part they now play within the dream of good and evil, of Love and anti-Love. You are here to build the New, to bring forth the heaven of living Love in which you are ever meant to live. Turn to Me and daily, moment by precious moment, I will show you who you are: a child of Love so beautiful that your cloak is made of stars, your heart is a living sun lighting up the darkness and revealing only light.

Give Me your Will, let Me lift you so you can see each moment the unity of Love. How all creation is My being and every part, magnificent and joyous, dances in a swirl of sweet exploding life. I will help you see beyond duality, beyond the veil within which lives the dream of separation being dreamed by My children. I Am only Love. And your heart is the key to the treasures held for you beyond time. Time—the illusory creation coming forth from "fitting into experience" a pendulum of good and bad experience.

Beloved ones, I speak to you whose hearts have known, have known deep inside that I would not create such a world as this you see before you. It can be easy to disengage, but you've lived the illusion for a long time. Thus can you assist each other in this. Assist each other in placing your attention on your hearts and using the power of Love you find there to infuse the world you want, not the world that's passing, the world of so much pain. You are co-creators. Made in My image, remember? It is true. You are made in My image and thus do you manifest the beliefs of your heart. Remember, the heart is where we are connected, so all the power, all the light, all the Love I pour to you comes directly and unfailingly to and through your heart. I Am Creator; I Am Love expanding through you.

And My covenant with you, My children, is that I shall always and forever grant your heart's desires. This is the promise given to each of you at the moment of your creation as children of the Love I Am. So if deep in your heart you are afraid, if you believe your heart is broken (pay attention to these words), if you are afraid that Love will hurt you, if you keep yourself protected, if you are waiting every moment for "the other shoe to drop," if you feel the world is hopeless, if you feel that life's not worth it, if you feel the world's about to end, be it from polluting it to death or from chaos and war, these deep "ways you feel" about your life–these are your heart's beliefs. And thus, beloved ones, **by our covenant** they shall manifest before you. For as the Love I Am comes pouring to you, whatever is held before the opening of your heart is what Love shall bring to life, shall help you co-create.

Thus you see that, if you stand before the White House with anger in your heart, with belief that nothing changes, that government is corrupt, and, worst of all, if you hold hatred there, within the temple of God that you are, then that, dear ones, is what you shall have more of.

You are the prize of the universe–the heart of God gone forth to create. There is really only Love to create with. But if you choose Love and anti-Love, you turn your face away from Love and, peering into the world you've made, you look for your identity. Oh, precious ones, don't find it there! Please wake into the truth of Love. Place your every resource with your true and glorious heart. I promise you that Love is the only power. And that, truly, it is the heart with which you shall always create what you experience, be it now, on Earth, or later, "after death." There is no progression, no good and bad, no better and best. There is only the truth of Love or the dream of separation.

If you can make this leap, you are those who bridge heaven and Earth, who begin to reclaim the paradise you never really left. But if you cannot, then please do continue on growing in your faith in Love. It is good to pray for peace, for even though it contains the belief in its opposite, for the moments you are focusing on Love you are using your co-creative consciousness to lift you ever closer to the unity of Love. It is best, however (and I use these terms because they are relevant here), it is the true way, the way that Jesus came to show you, to see only Love. To place every bit of the power of your heart upon the paradise of Love that this Earth is in truth, giving none of your energy to the illusion that I can ever create anything but Love.

Do you see? Do you see how this must be a fantasy if in Me darkness does not exist? If I Am All That Is, which I Am, then nowhere in Creation is there anything but Love. Oh, dear ones, this I promise you. You were created in Love; made as a glorious reproduction of what I Am as Creator. You thus came forth, truly, as Twin Flames, the forces of the Divine. Ocean of Love, Divine Feminine, and the great movement of My Will upon it, Divine Masculine. Born as one with two points of conscious Love, you forever exist in a grand unity of Love, sparking together to co-create more Love.

I call you home. Home to the unity of Love I Am and that you are in Me. Every thought for peace, every prayer has value, and every act of service in Love's name to another is a star in the night of this "pocket of duality." But the real service for which many of you have come is to join together, heart after heart, in the conviction of the truth of only Love and, forming a net of your great auras of light, to lift the world free of the reversal caused by humanity's belief in good and evil.

Thank you, beloved one, for reading this. Do you feel My living presence in your heart? Do you see the light behind these words, the packages of Love I now deliver? Then you are called, beloved one. Called to remember a world of only Love. Called to place this vision before you until it sinks into your heart and becomes your one desire: to return to My children their birthright. You have angels all around you. Your hands are being held, finger of light to finger of light, by the masters who go before you to pave the way. Your every affirmation of the world of Love you choose is heralded by archangels as they trumpet across the heavens, "A child of God awakes! A child of God awakes!" And choruses of beings, living stars greater than your sun, carry forth the message that the whole of Love I Am is filled with rejoicing. For every child of God who returns heals those many lives of the dreams of anti-Love that sprang forth from their creative heart. And the whole of the cosmos is glad, because a hole in My heart, caused by your facing away into "darkness," is healed. The heart of God is mended, ah, but more than this: the Love I Am goes forth again as you to create new things for us to love together.

I Am calling. You can hear Me. It won't be long now, beloved ones.

ABOUT YAEL AND DOUG POWELL
AND CIRCLE OF LIGHT

Yael and Doug Powell live at Circle of Light, their spiritual center in Eureka Springs, Arkansas, that looks out over Beaver Lake and the Ozark Mountains. Both Yael and Doug are ordained ministers, and the lovely Chapel at Circle of Light is the frequent scene of beautiful sacred weddings.

Yael spends a good deal of her time in bed as a result of pain from a severe physical disability. Her "up-time" is spent officiating at weddings or receiving the Messages from God in meditation. Doug is an artist and skilled craftsman at pottery and woodworking. If it is windy, you'll definitely find him at his lifelong passion–sailing! Shanna Mac Lean, compiler and editor of the Messages, also lives at Circle of Light. She can usually be found on the phone or at the computer.

Completing the Circle of Light family are their wonderful animal companions. Christos (boy) and Angel (girl) are their two beloved Pomeranians. Ariel (Duff Duff) is a pure white cat who has been with Yael and Doug for 17 years. He mostly frequents the garden and occasionally attends a wedding. Then there is Magic Cat, of course with his entourage–his SoulMate, Magic's Love (Love, for short); and their sister Sweetheart, Shanna's "Sweetie." These babies celebrated their first birthday on July 24, 2004, and it would be no exaggeration to say that they rule the household. All of our animals are very loved!

CIRCLE OF LIGHT ORDER FORM
SAY 'YES' TO LOVE SERIES

Please send the following:

——copies of *God Explains Soulmates* @ $11 ———($3 S&H)
——copies of *God Unveils SoulMate Love & Sacred Sexuality* @ $19.95
——— ($3.50 S&H)
——copies of *God's Guidance to LightWorkers* @ $14 ———($3 S&H)
——copies of *God leads Humanity Toward Christ Consciousness* @ $16
——— ($3 S&H)
——copies of *Magic Cat Explains Creation!* @ $16 ———($3 S&H)
——copies of *Giving Birth to the Christ Light* @ $16 ——— ($3 S&H)

Prices are for the USA. For more than one book, reduce S&H by $1 per book or contact us. For postage to other countries, please email us first and we will find the best shipping cost.

Name:_____

Address:_____

City:_____

State:_____ Zip Code:_____

To use credit cards, please go to our web site www.circleoflight.net OR you may fax your order with credit card to (479) 253-2880.

Name on Card:_____

CC#:_____ Exp. Date:_____

If you would like to be on our email list and receive bi-monthly Messages from God, please fill out the following:

Email address:_____

Circle of Light
3969 Mundell Road, Eureka Springs, Arkansas 72631
www.circleoflight.net
connect@circleoflight.net
1-866-629-9894 Toll Free
or 479-253-6832, 2774